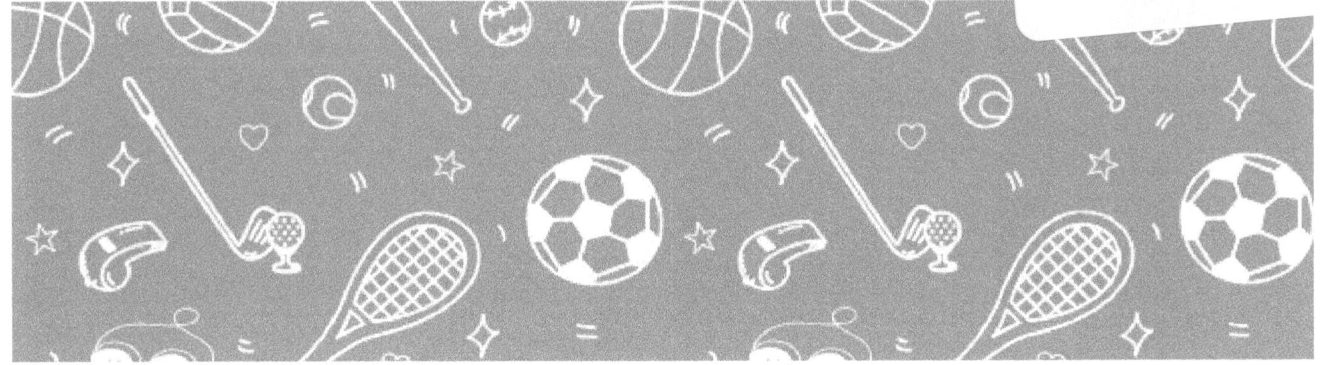

ISBN: 979-8-9870266-2-5

For more books or information,
visit Empower Books online at empowerbooksforkids.net

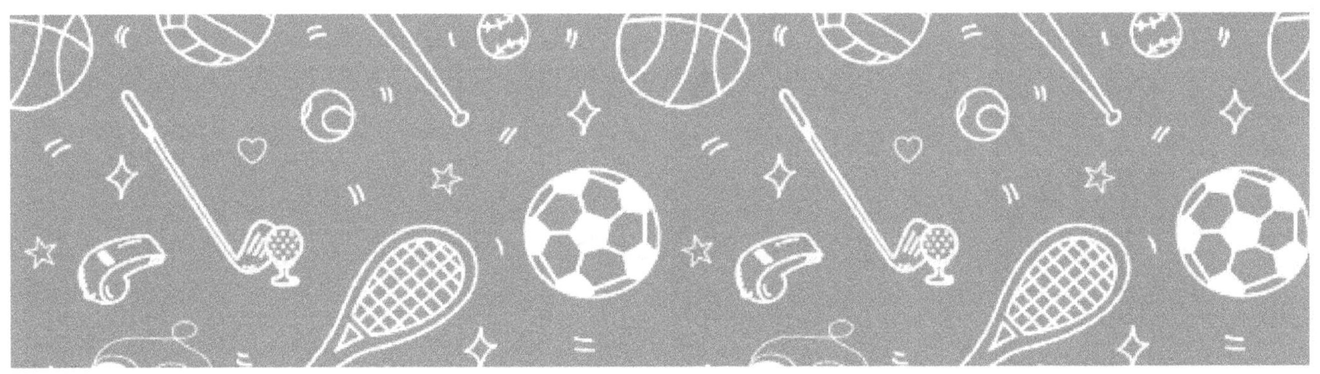

This book belongs to:

You can accomplish all things. Keep believing in yourself, keep working hard and continue to follow your dreams.

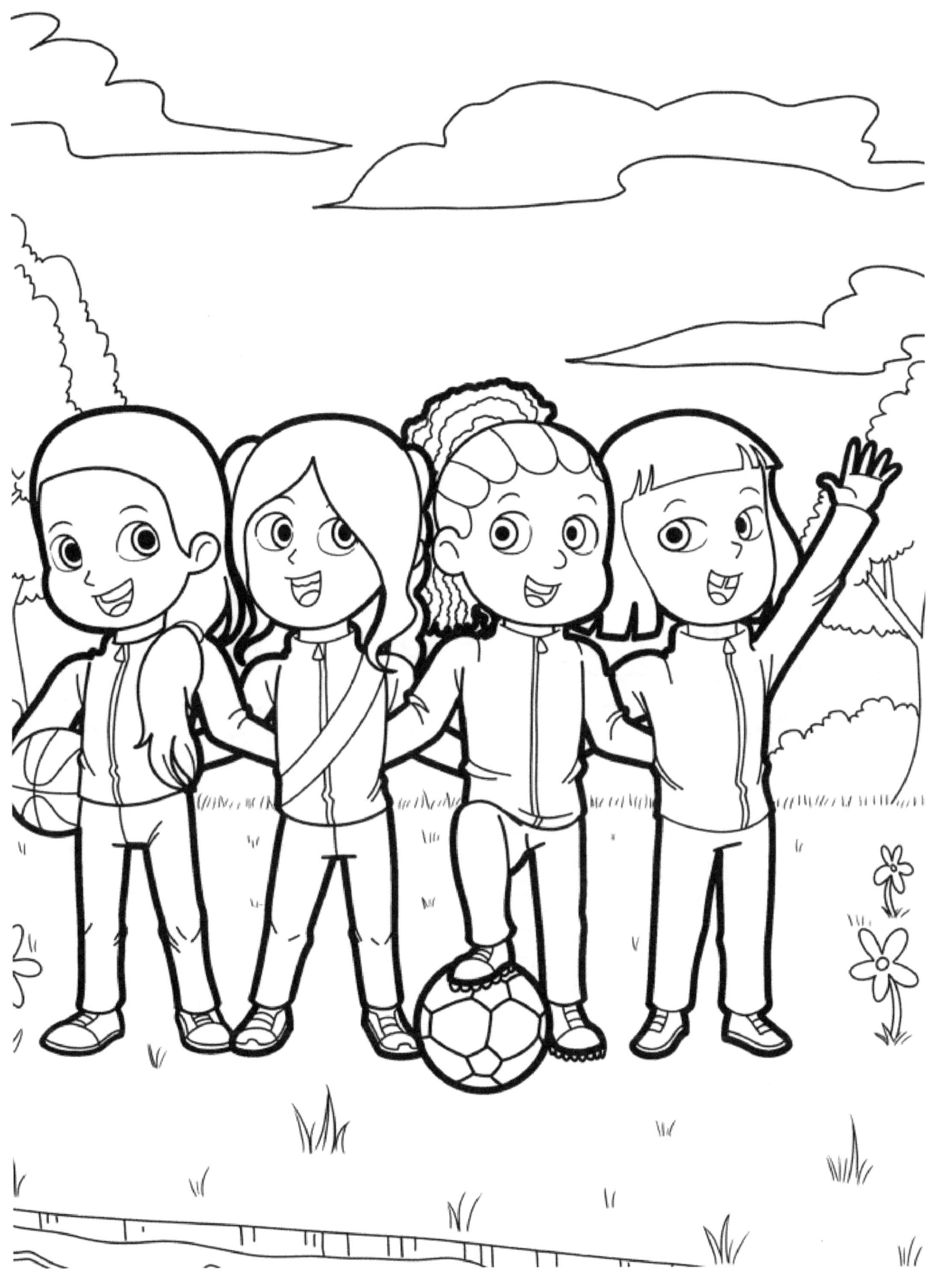

Can you name and color each sport below?

1.

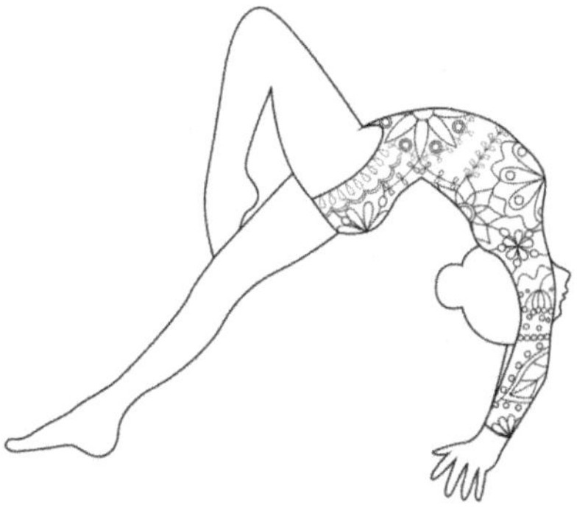

2.

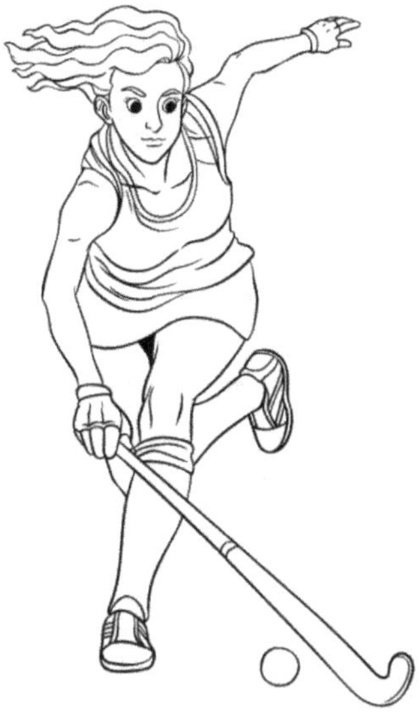

3.

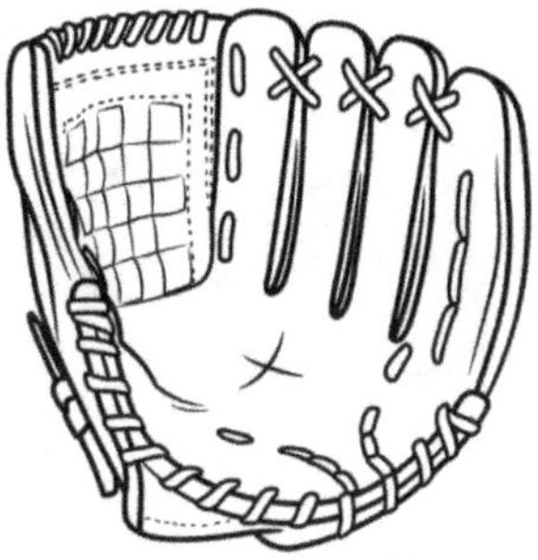

4.

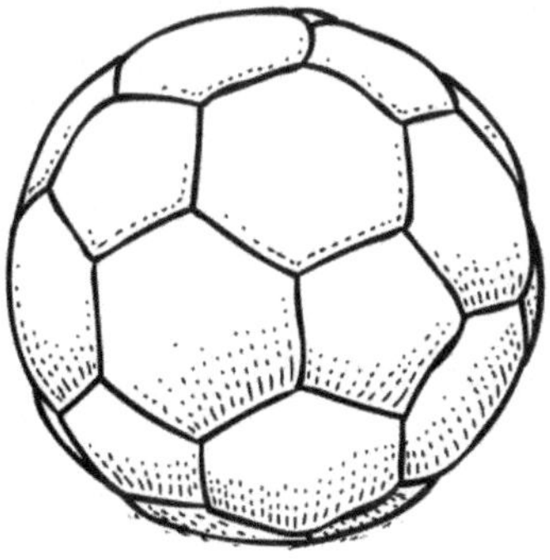

5.

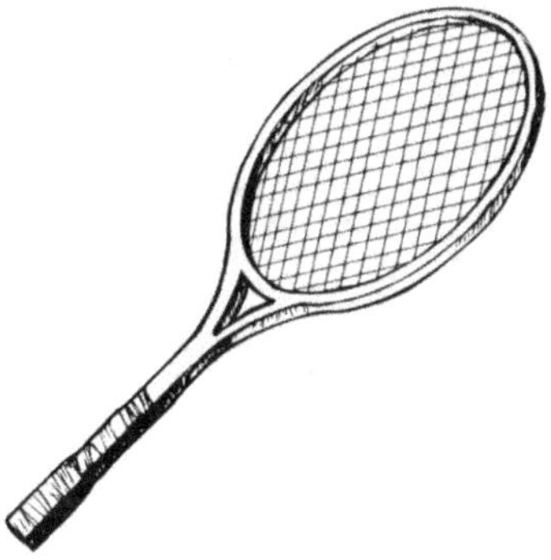

1.Gymnastics 2. Field Hockey 3. Softball 4. Soccer 5. Tennis

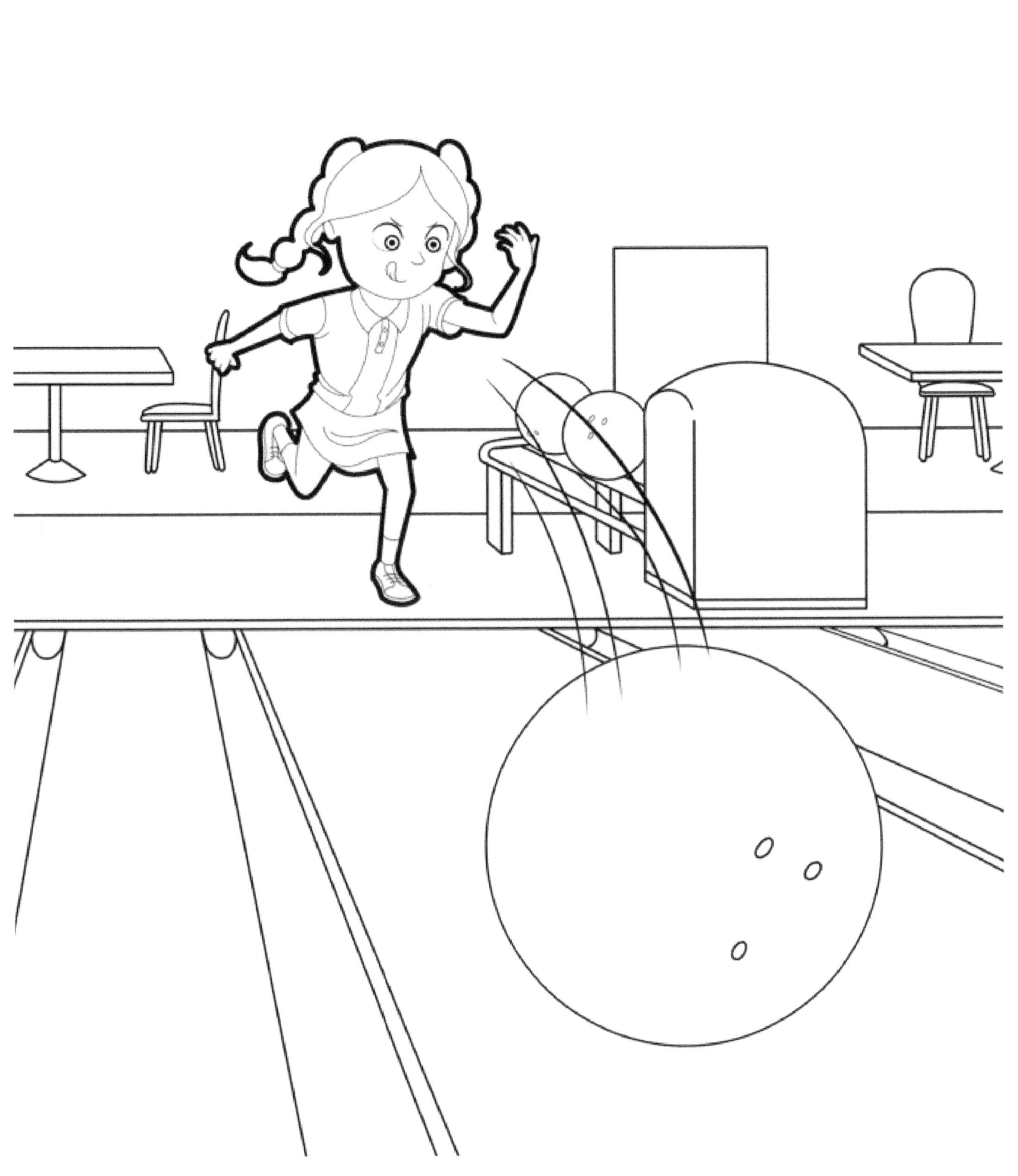

Can you find the soccer ball?

Start

Finish

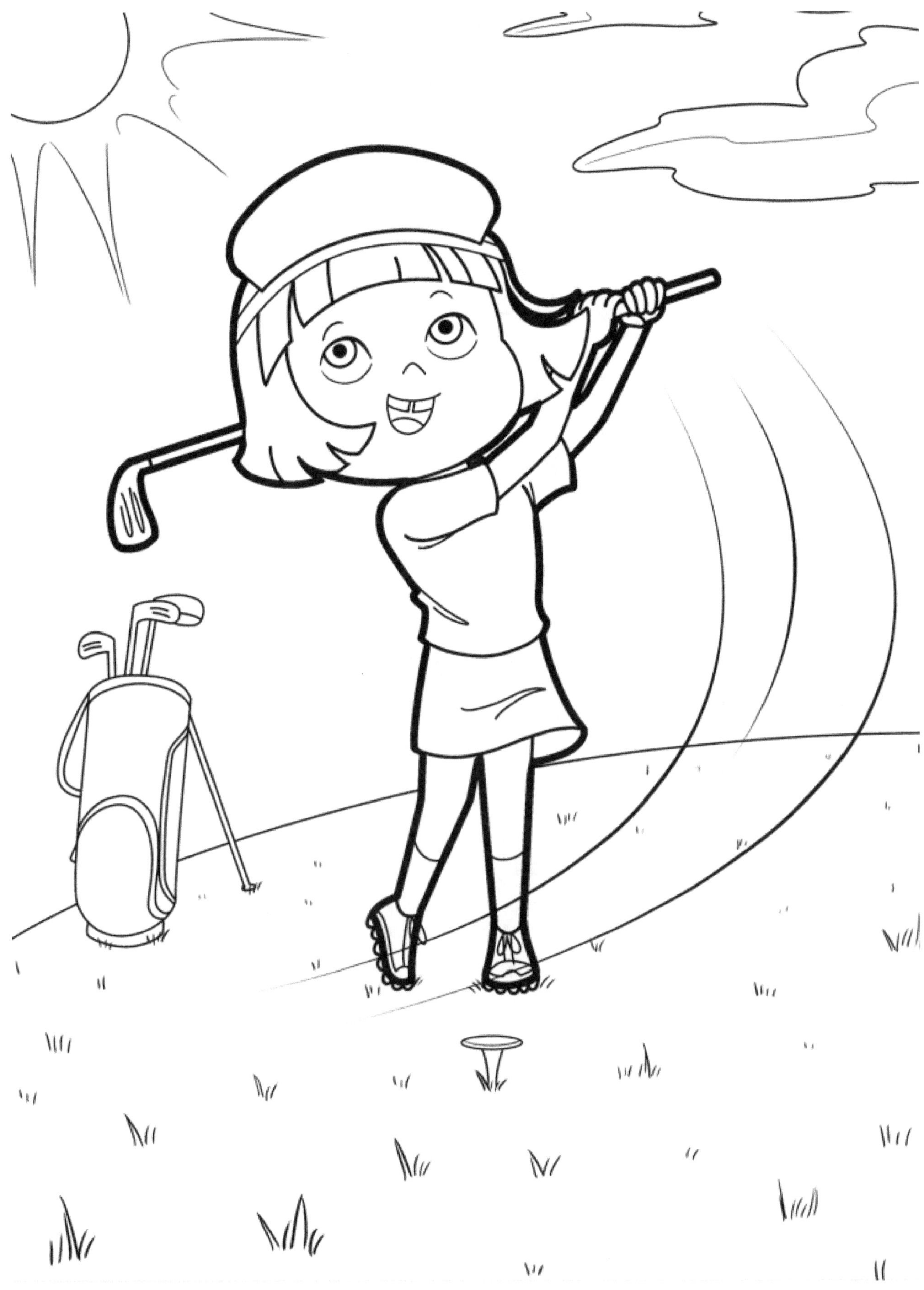

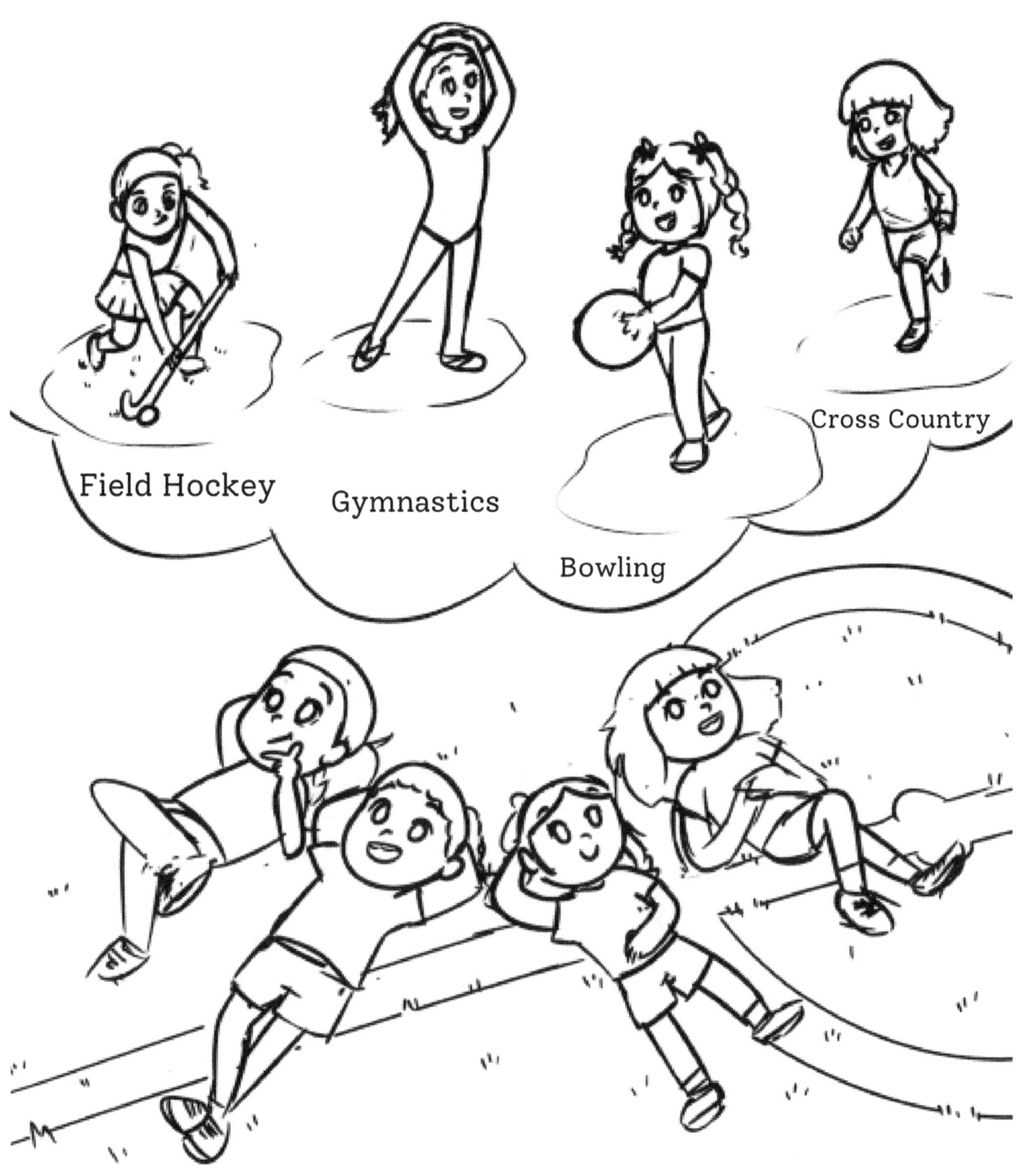

What sport do you think about playing?

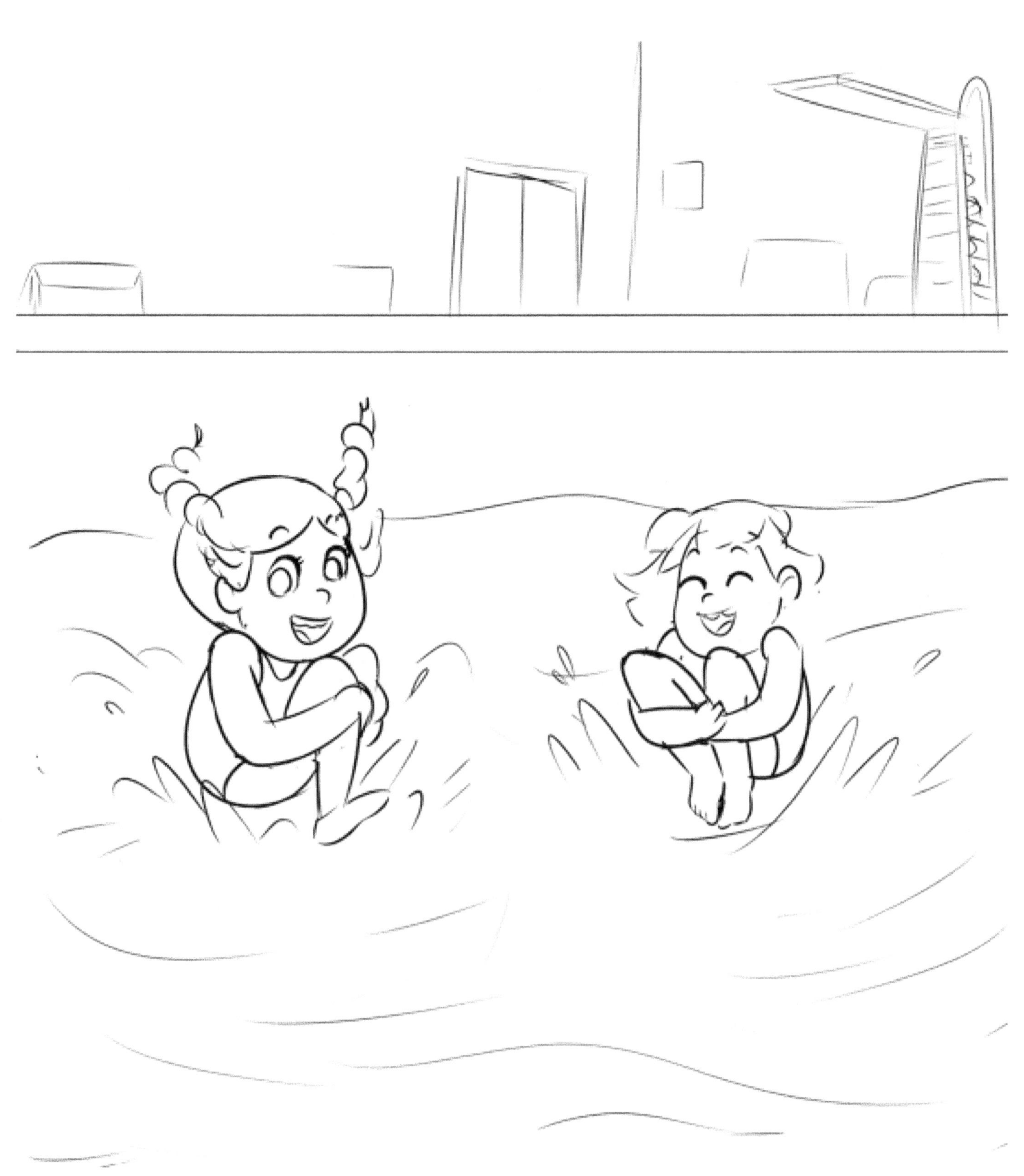

Can you find the hidden words?

Z	A	Y	P	O	W	I	N
N	L	H	S	D	E	P	P
M	Q	E	C	I	V	T	R
B	U	A	O	C	P	E	A
P	G	L	R	F	J	A	C
L	I	T	E	I	C	M	T
A	V	H	H	R	T	X	I
Y	Q	Y	J	N	J	H	C
A	X	Q	Y	P	W	K	E
S	T	R	O	N	G	C	Q
C	W	O	Y	F	U	N	C

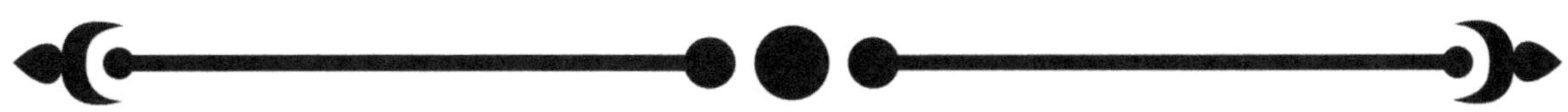

Strong
Team

Fun
Score

Play
Win

Healthy
Practice

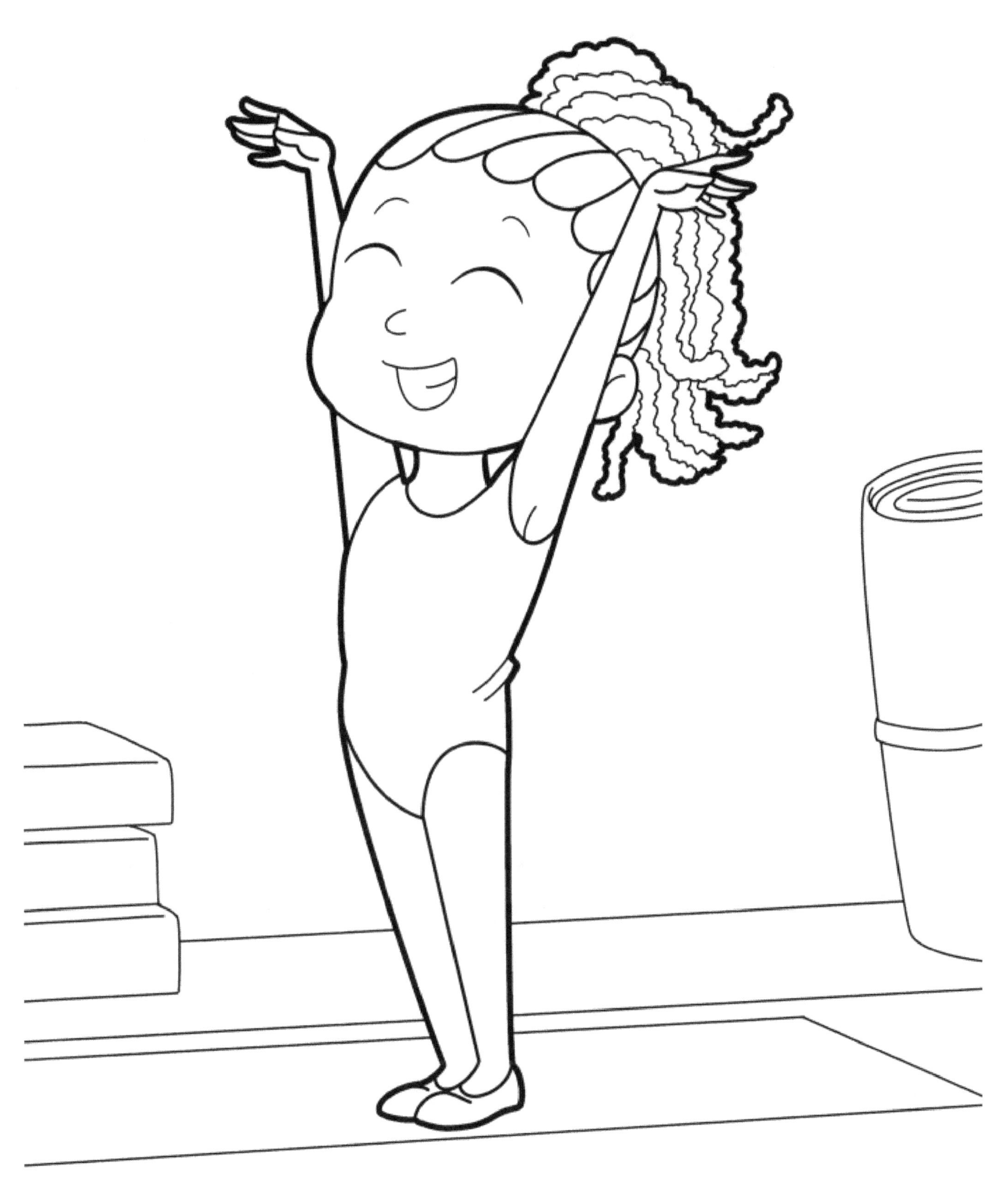

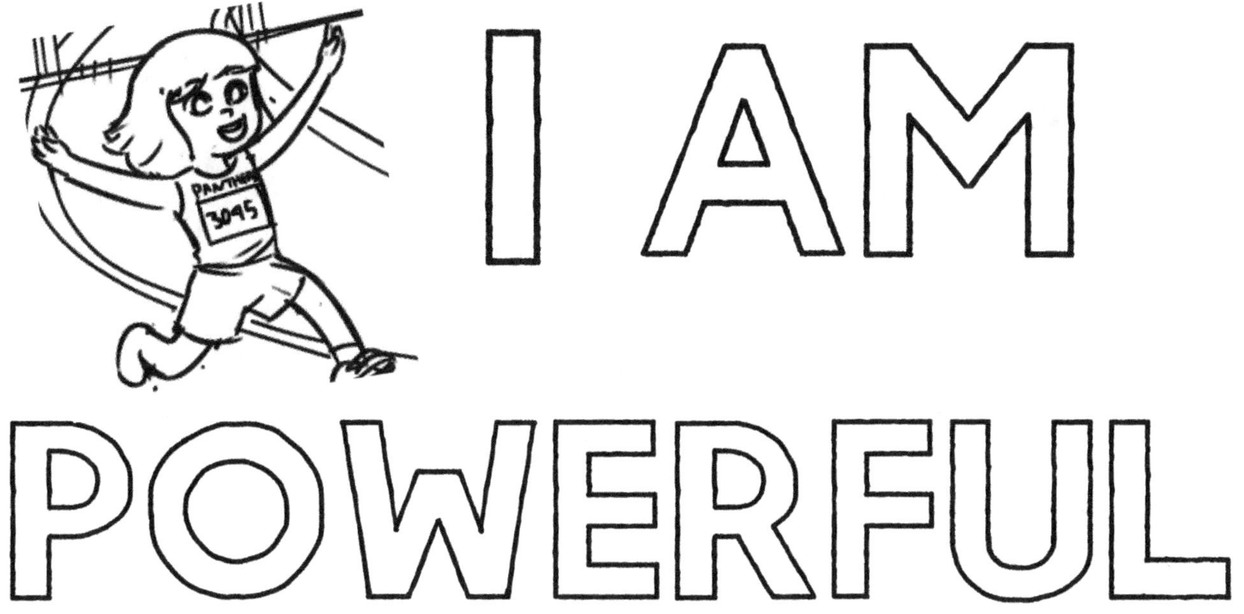

Draw a picture of you in the rectangle!

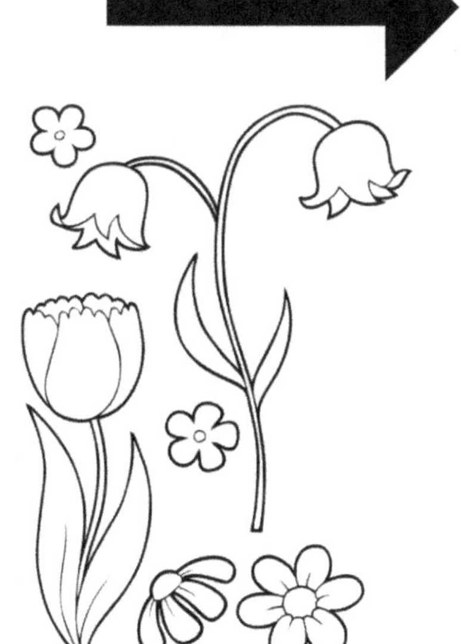

You are powerful!

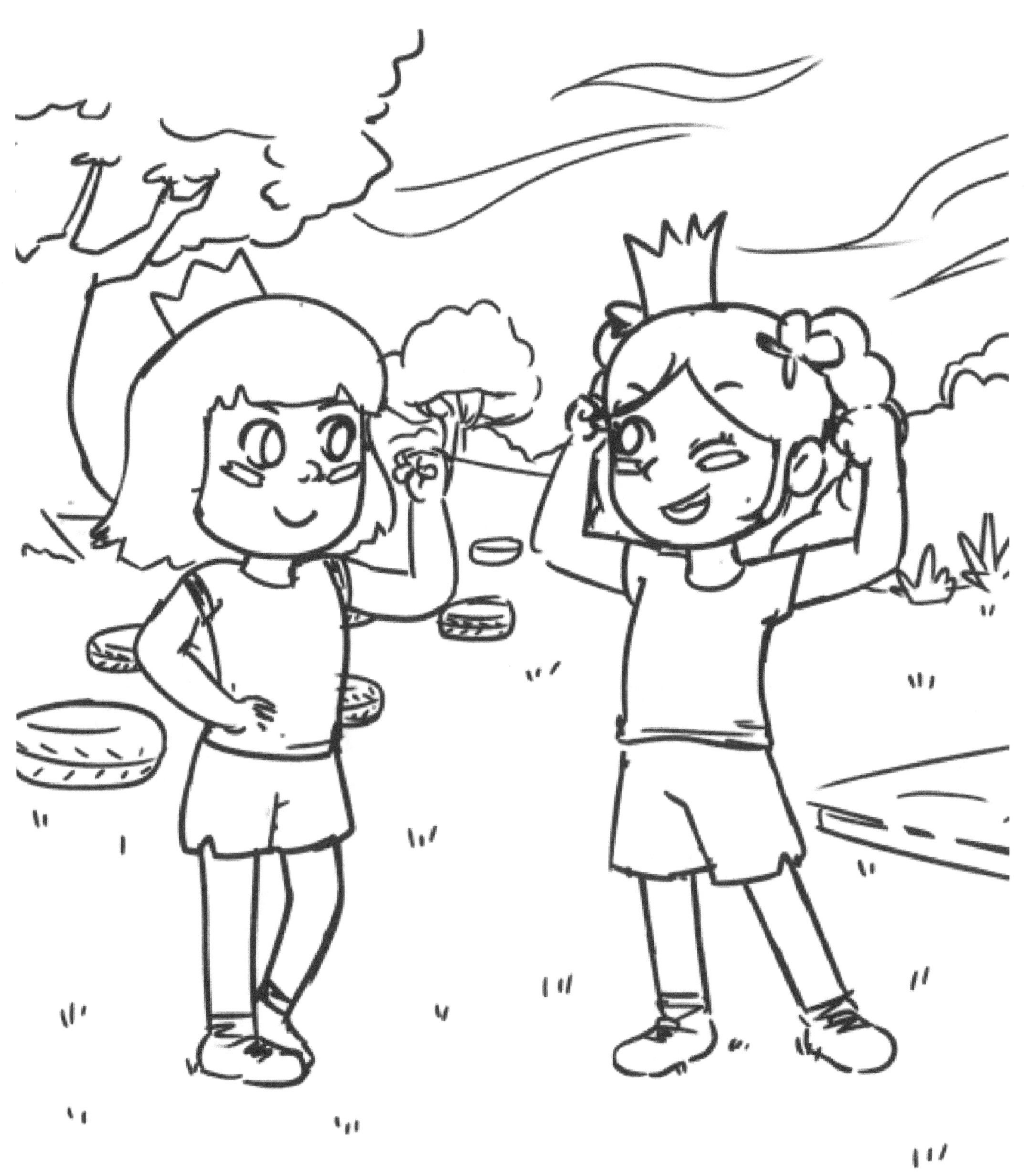

Girls are strong and tough!

Count the images and write the number on the blank line.

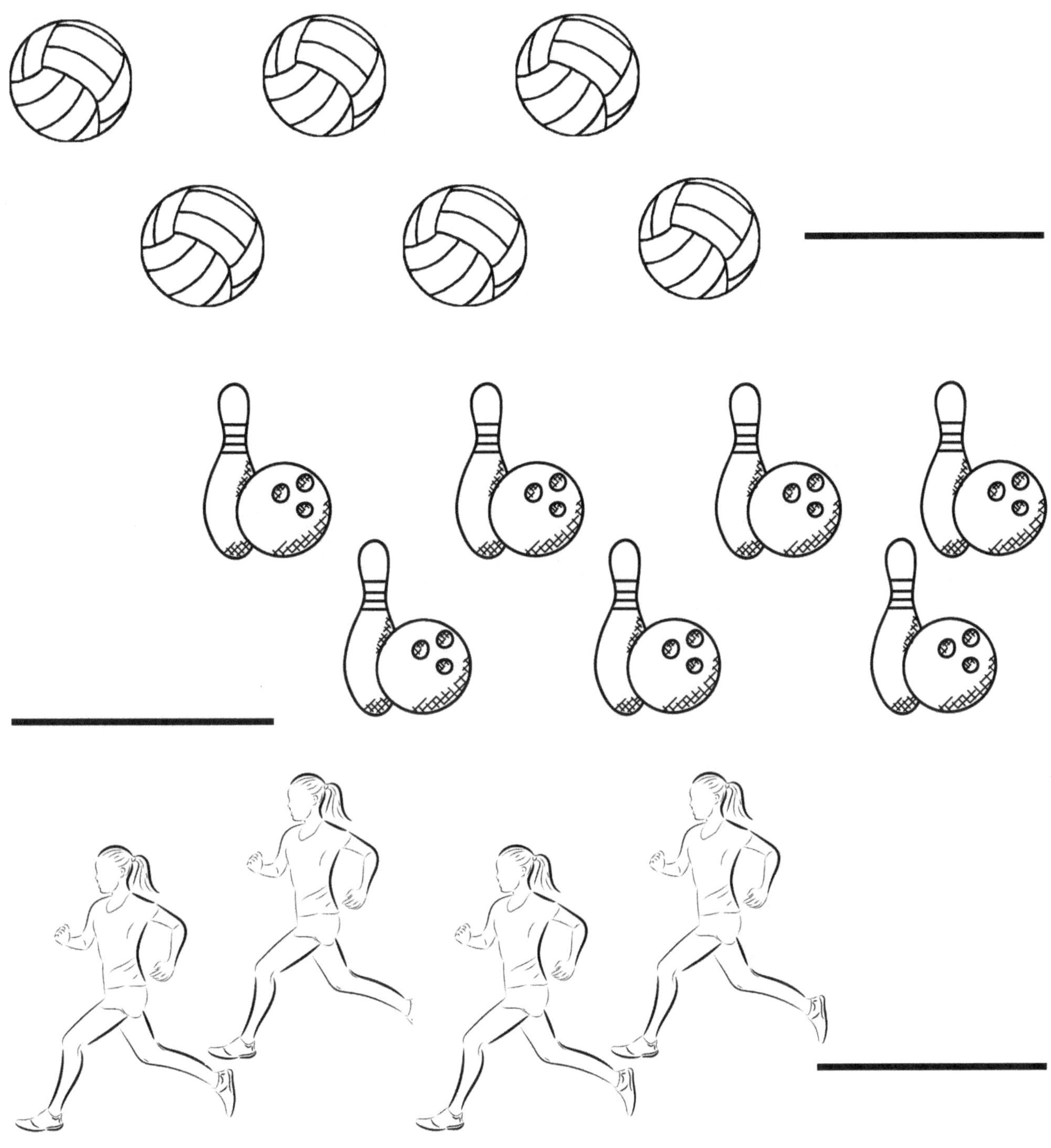

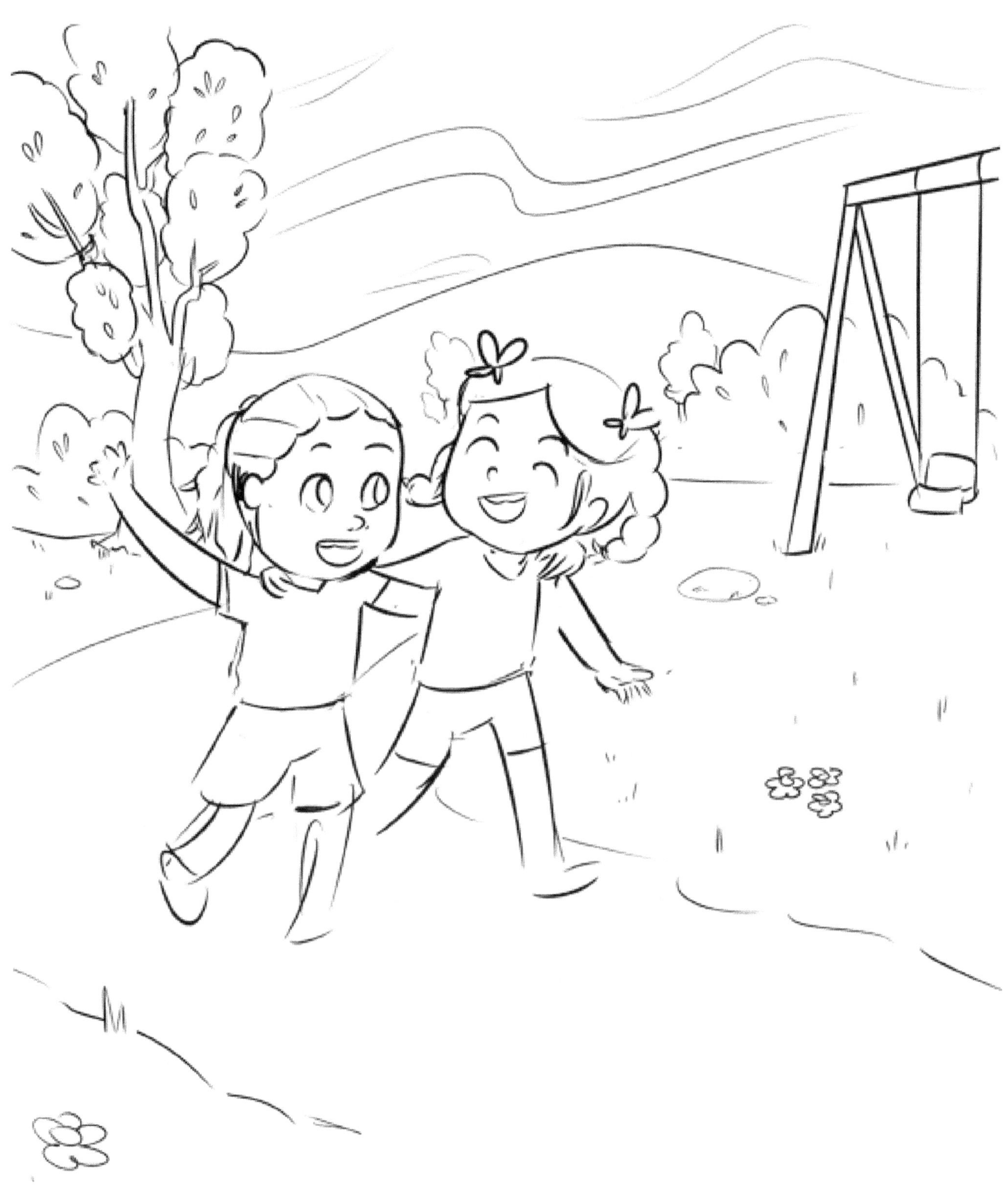

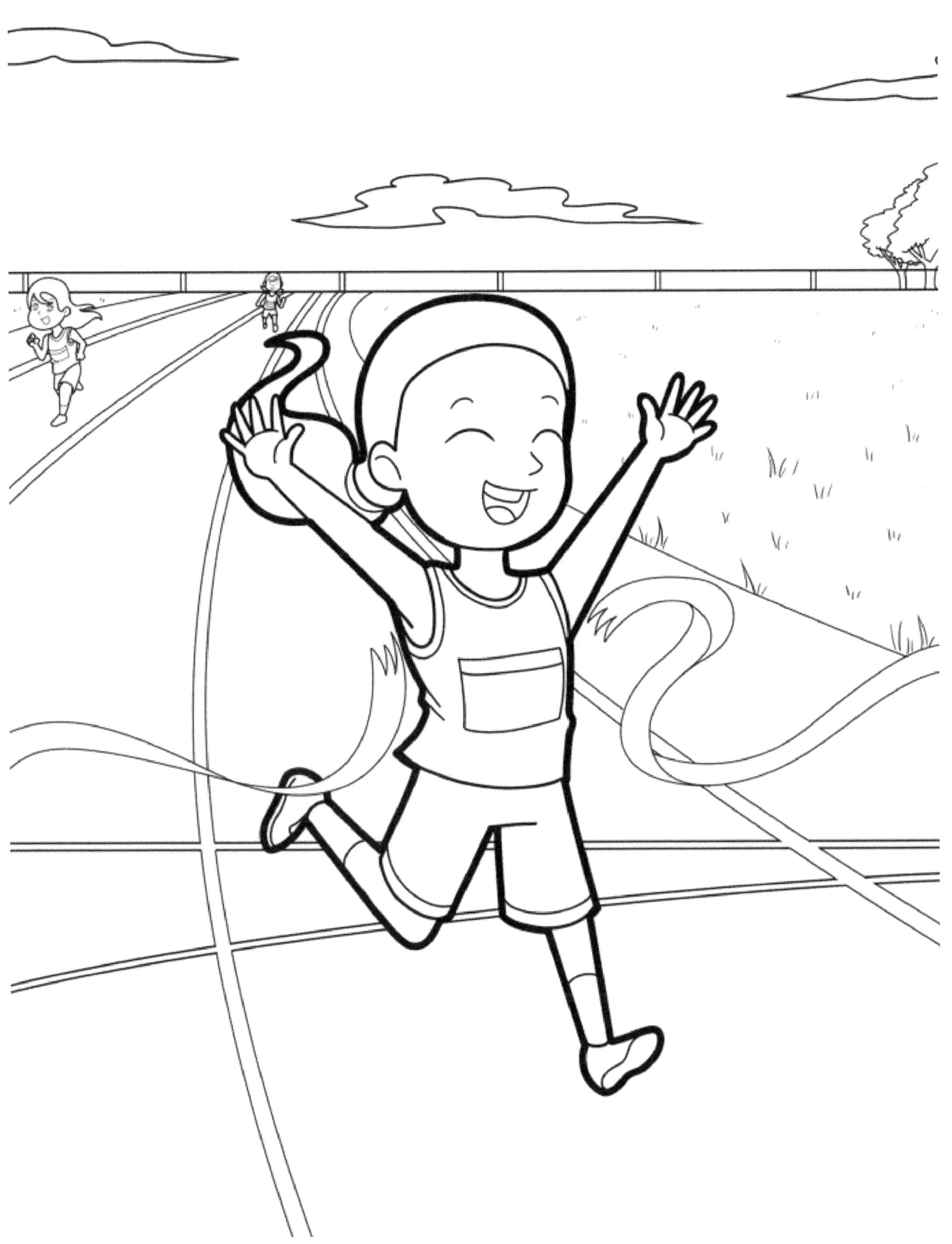

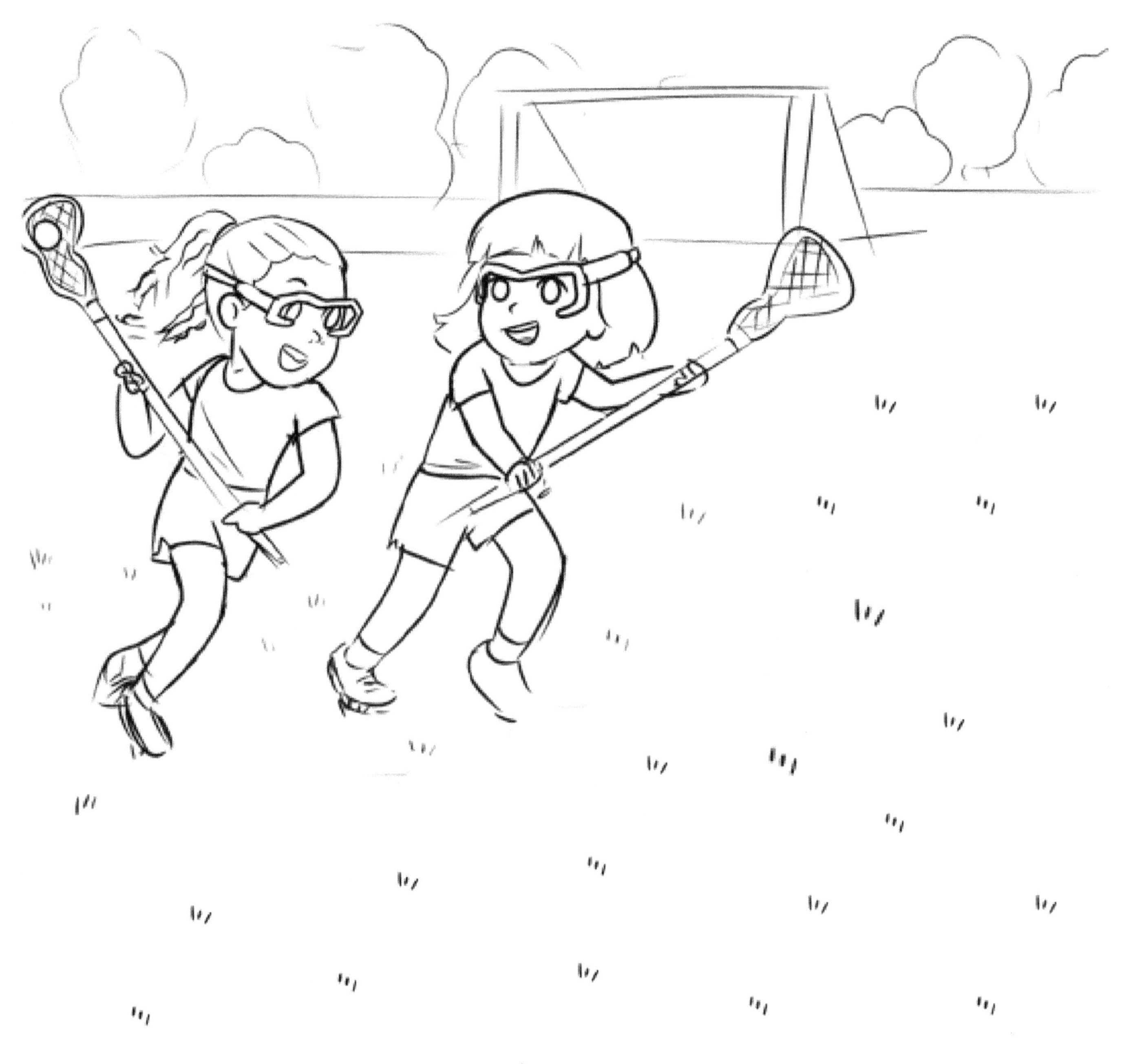

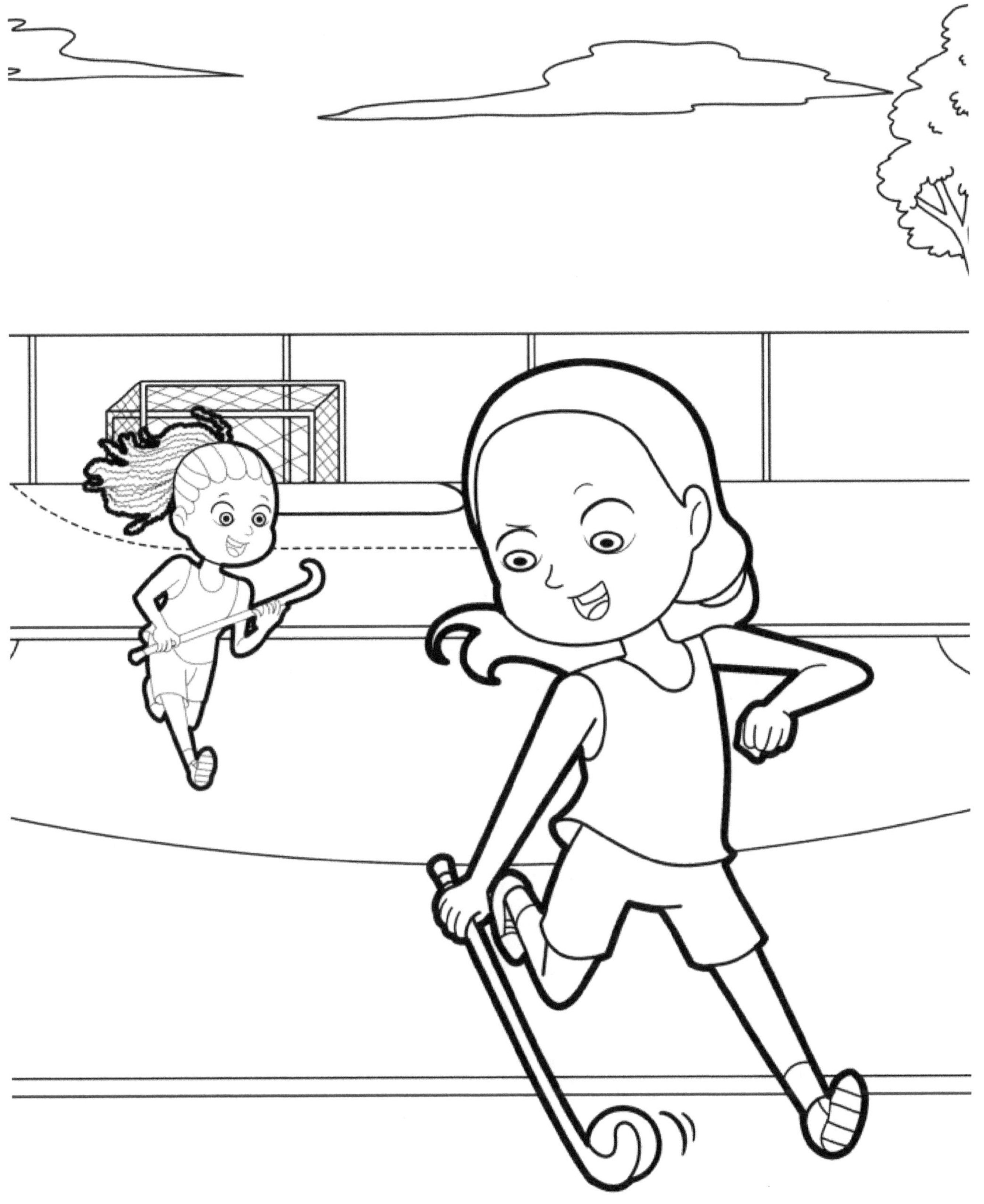

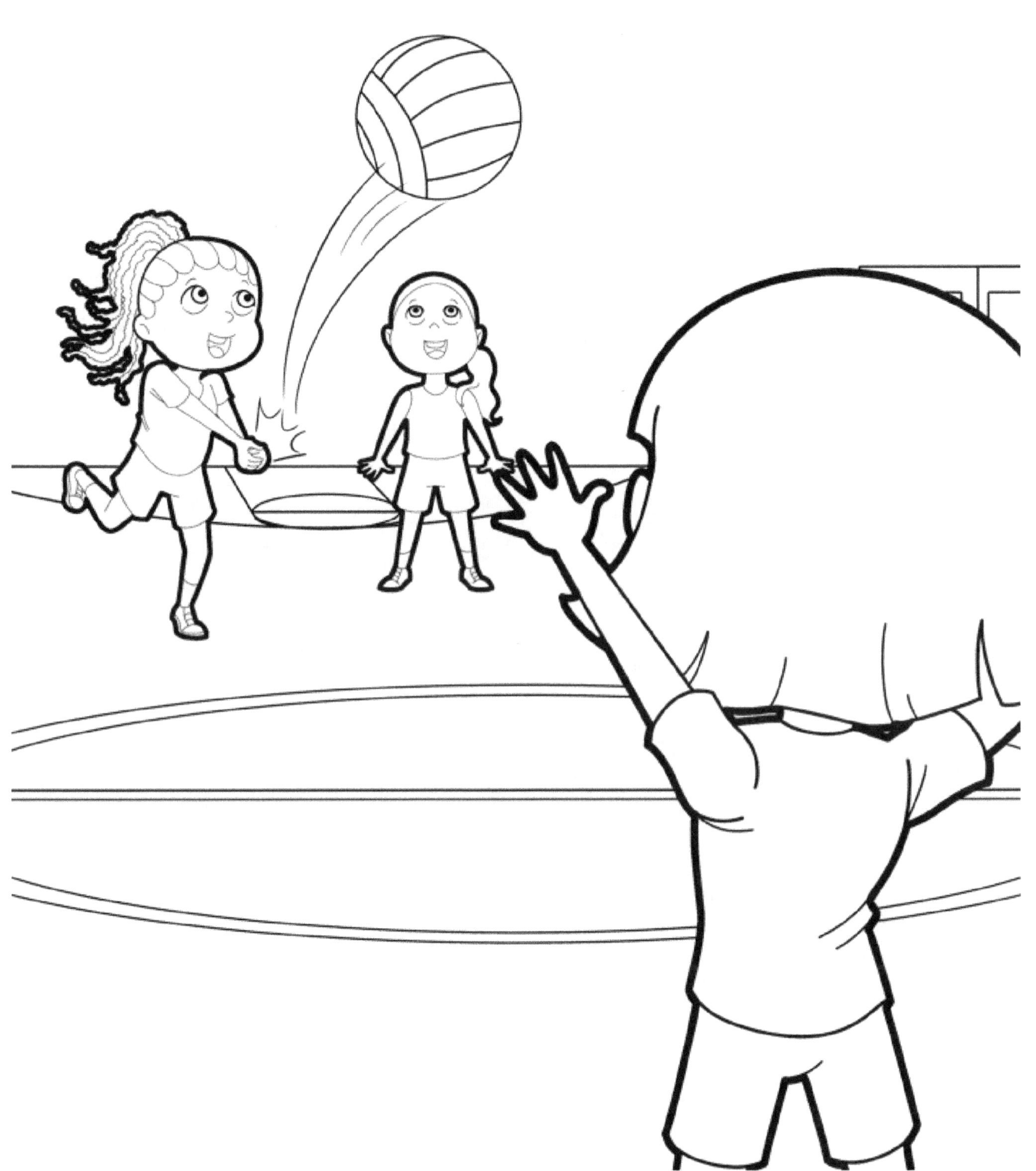

Practice writing the word below.

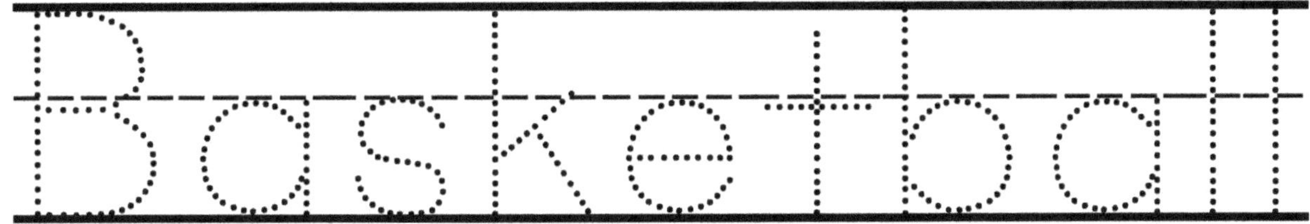

Color the girl playing basketball with your own style!

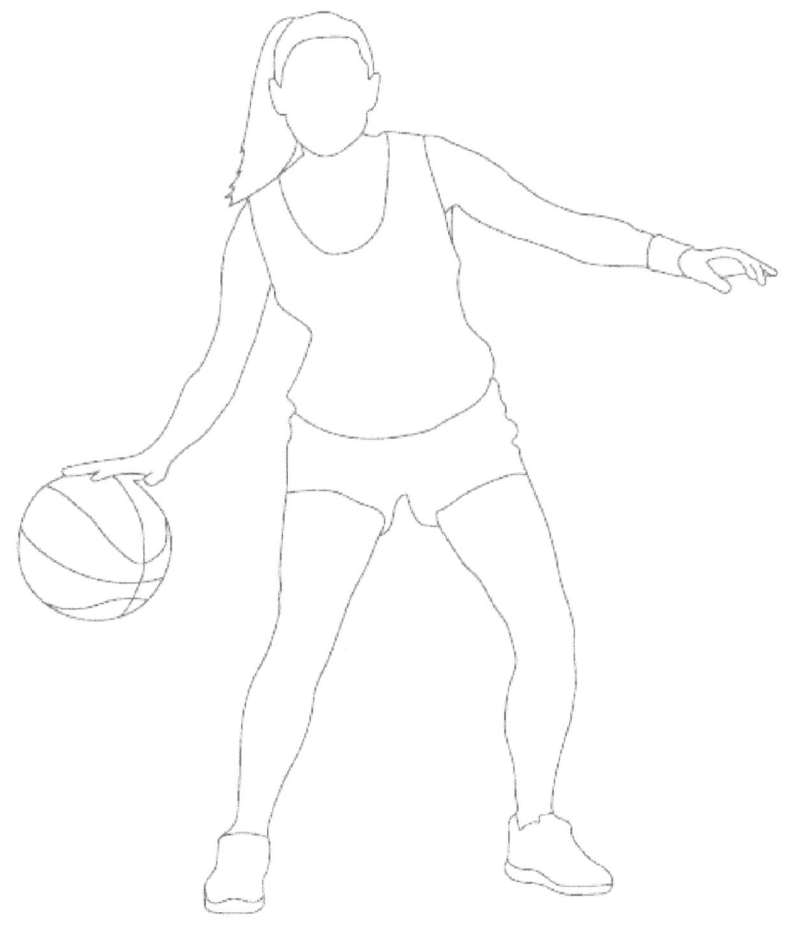

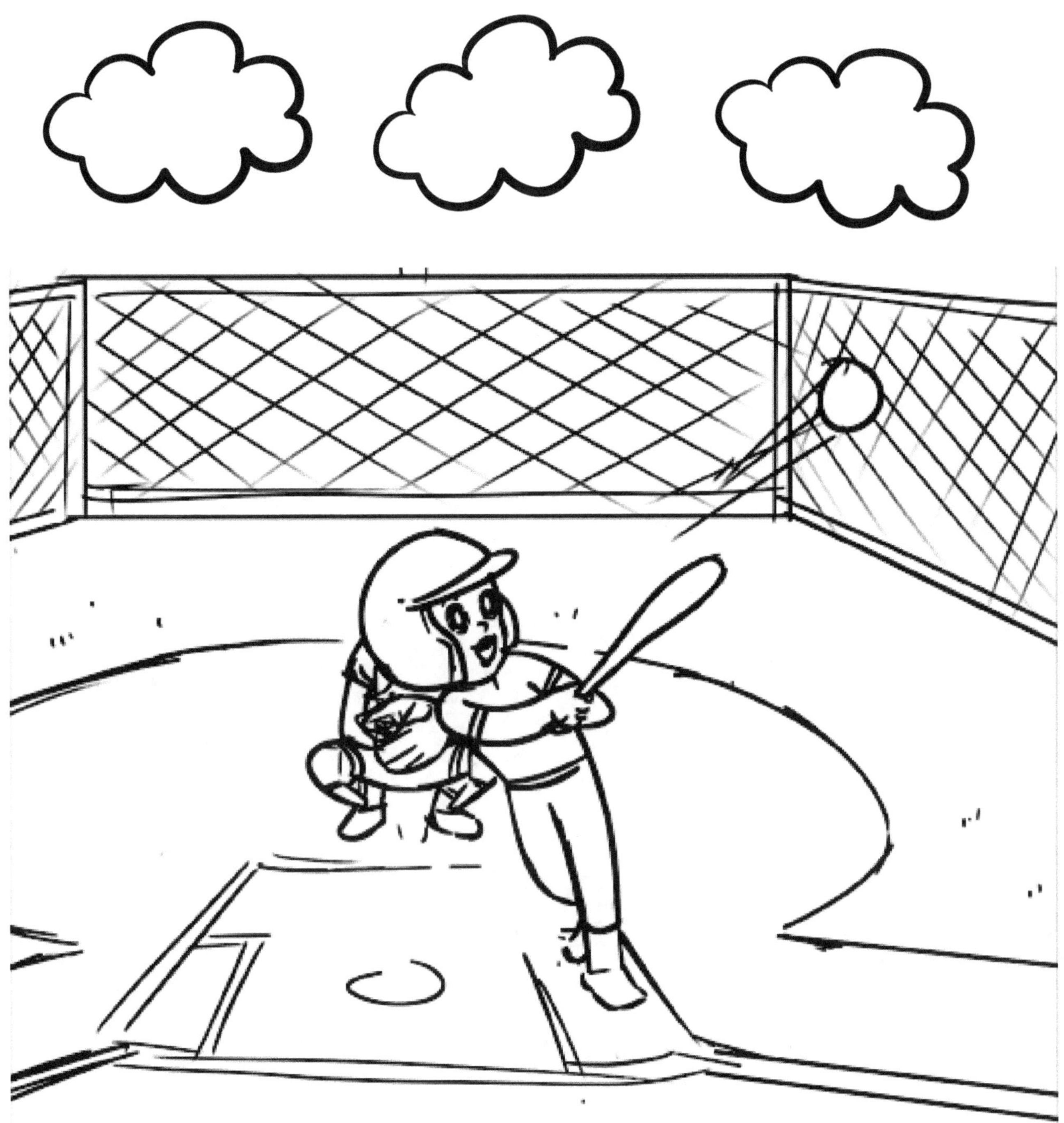

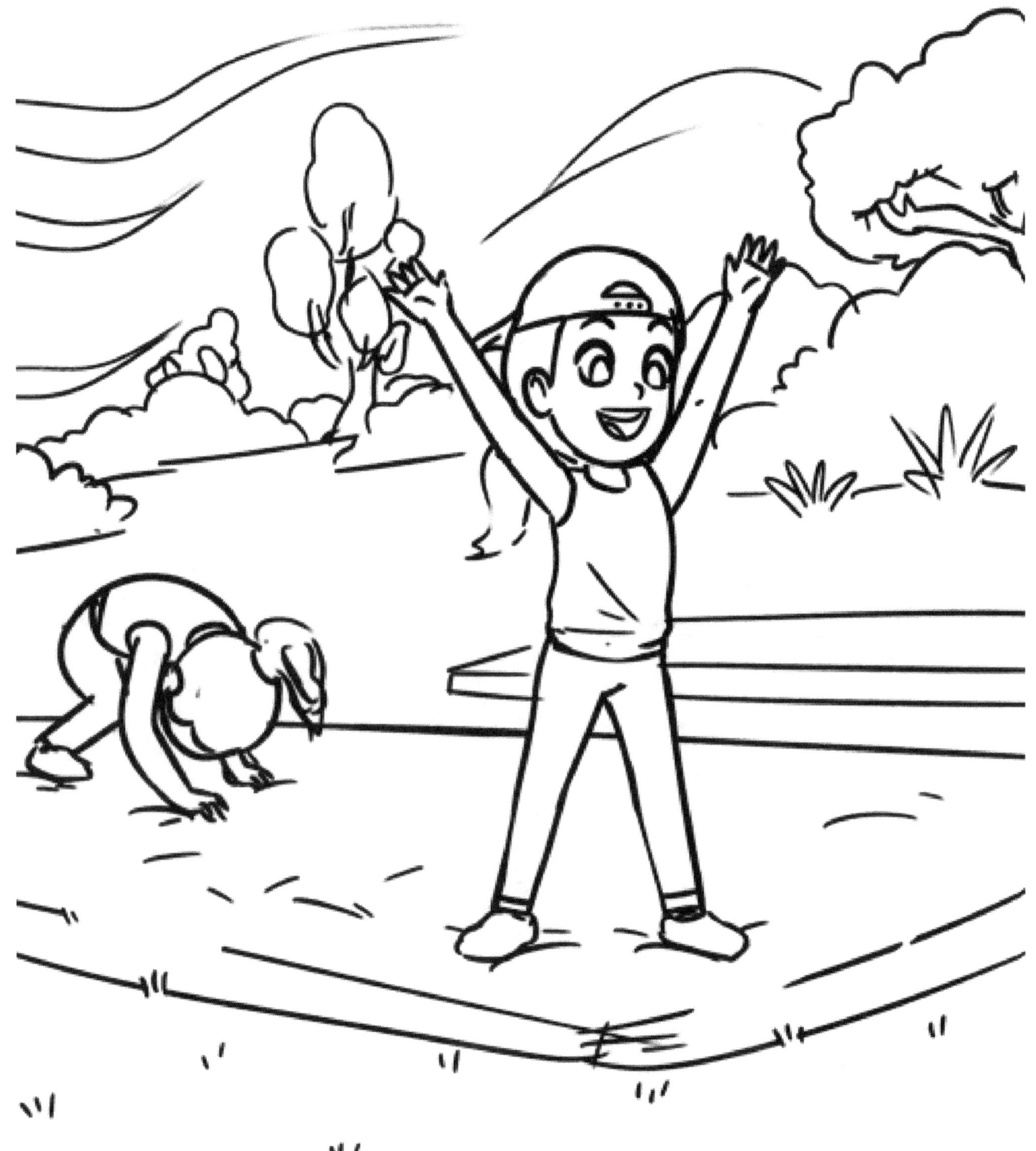

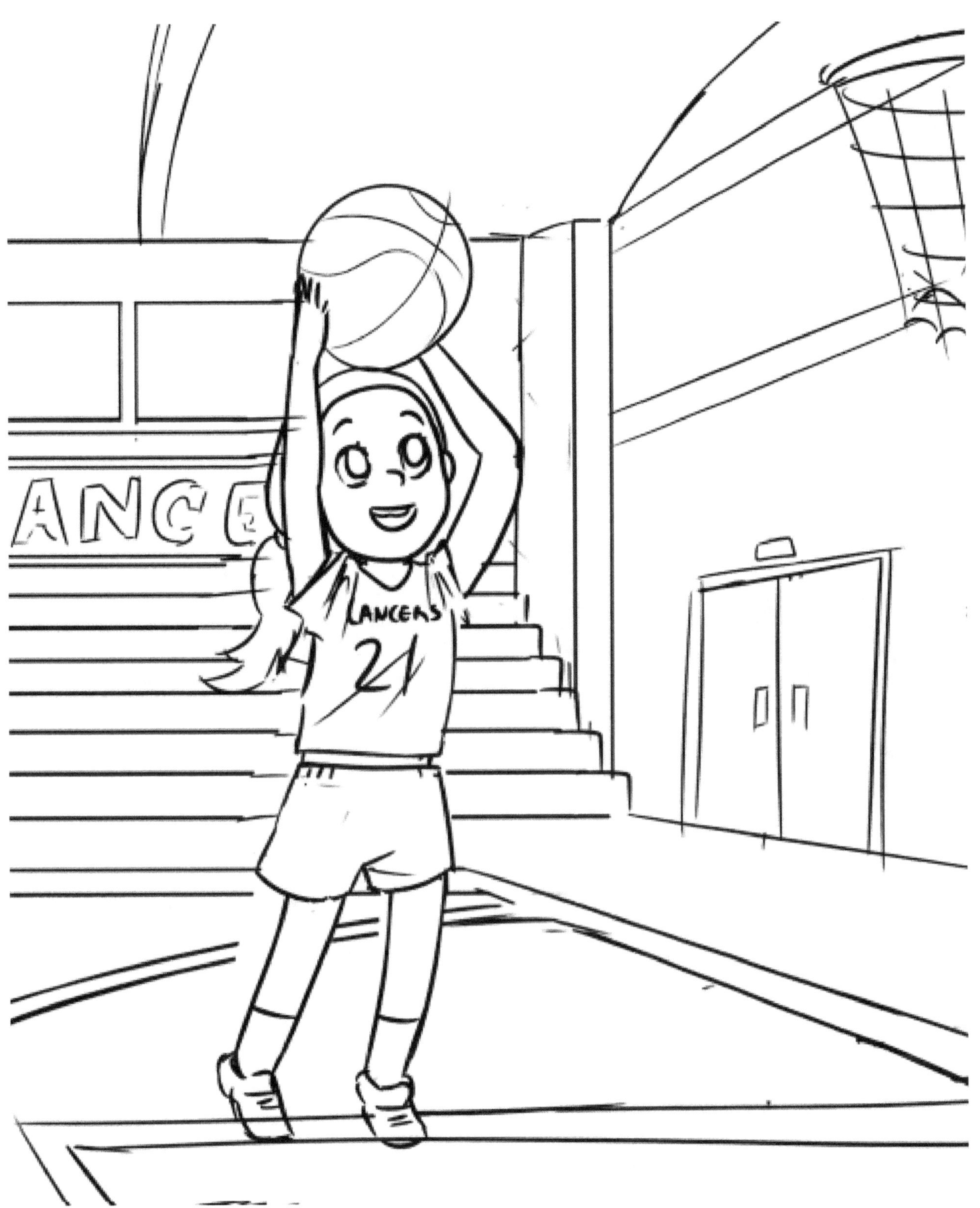
ANCE
LANCERS
21

You can be friends with the "Girls Can!" squad!

Draw a picture of yourself in the rectangle

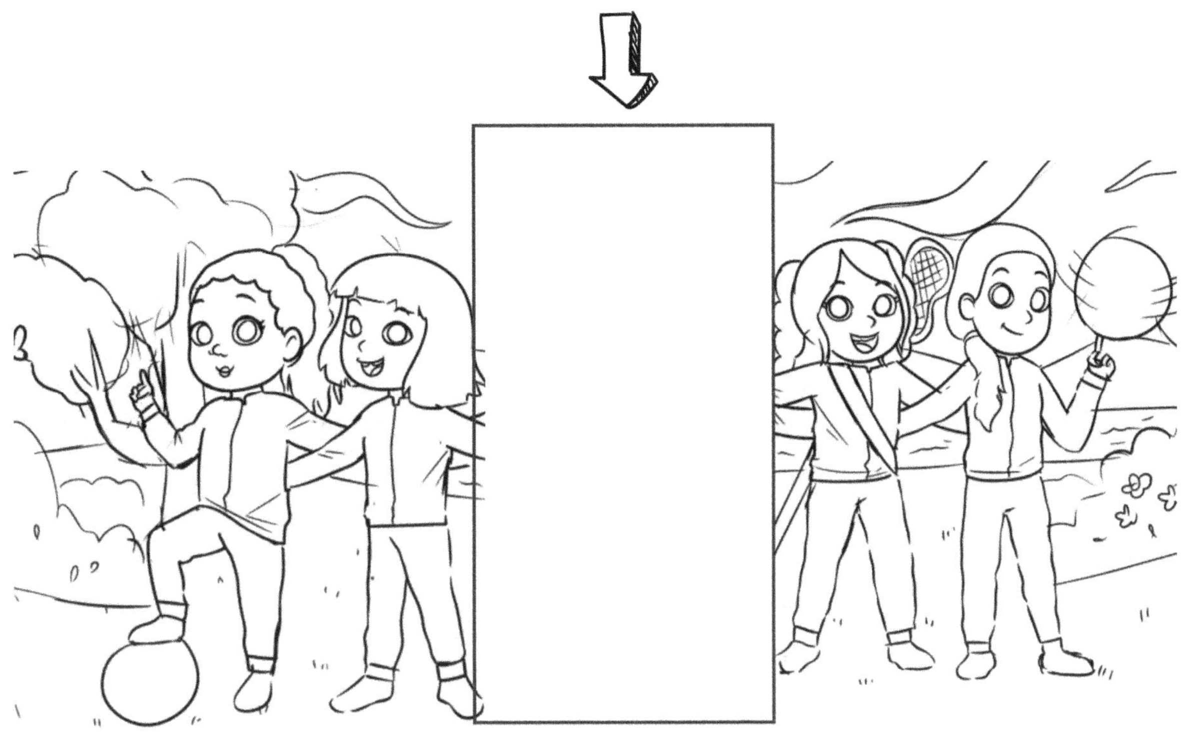

____

Jade Mei ⇧ Luna Allie

Write your name!

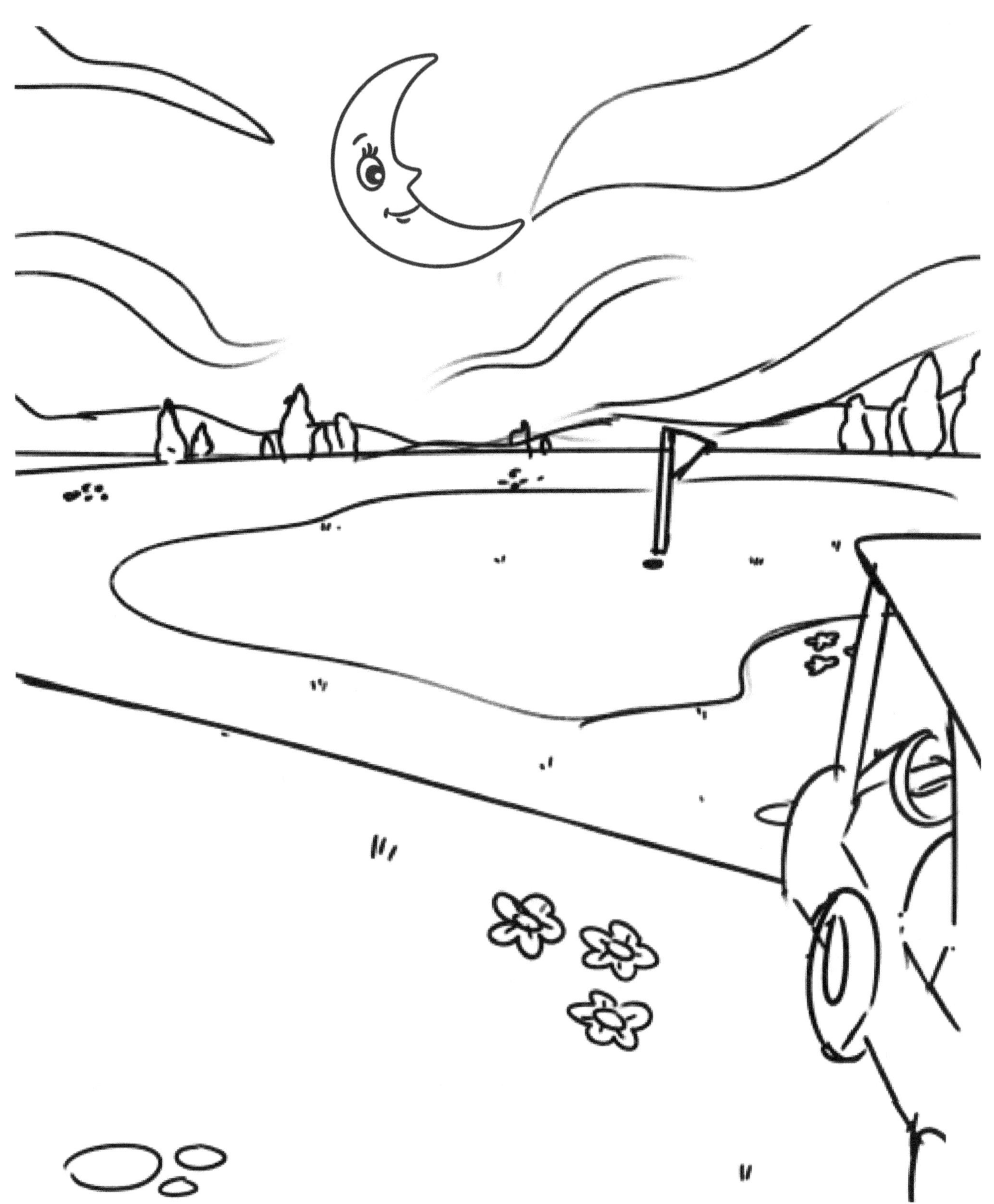

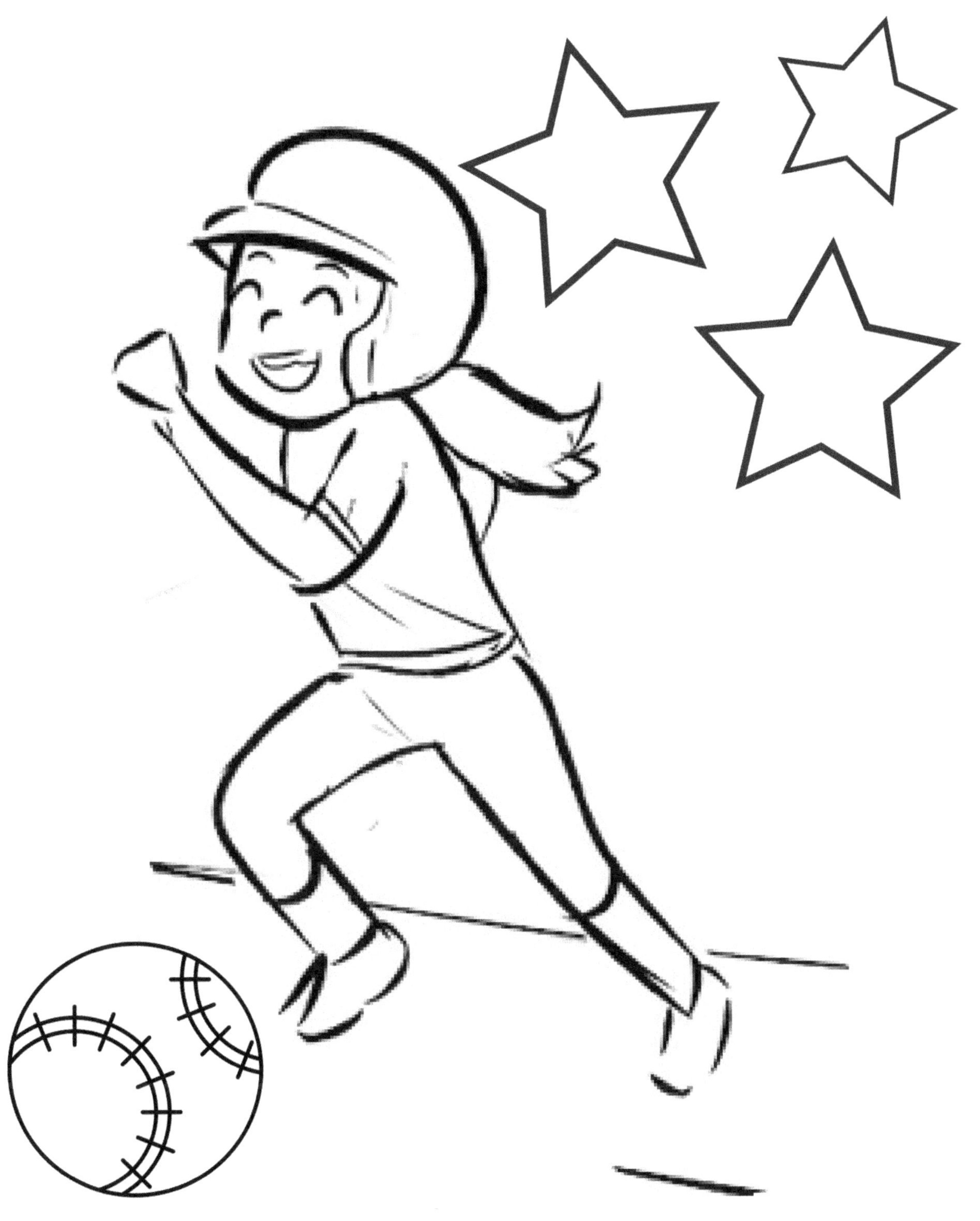

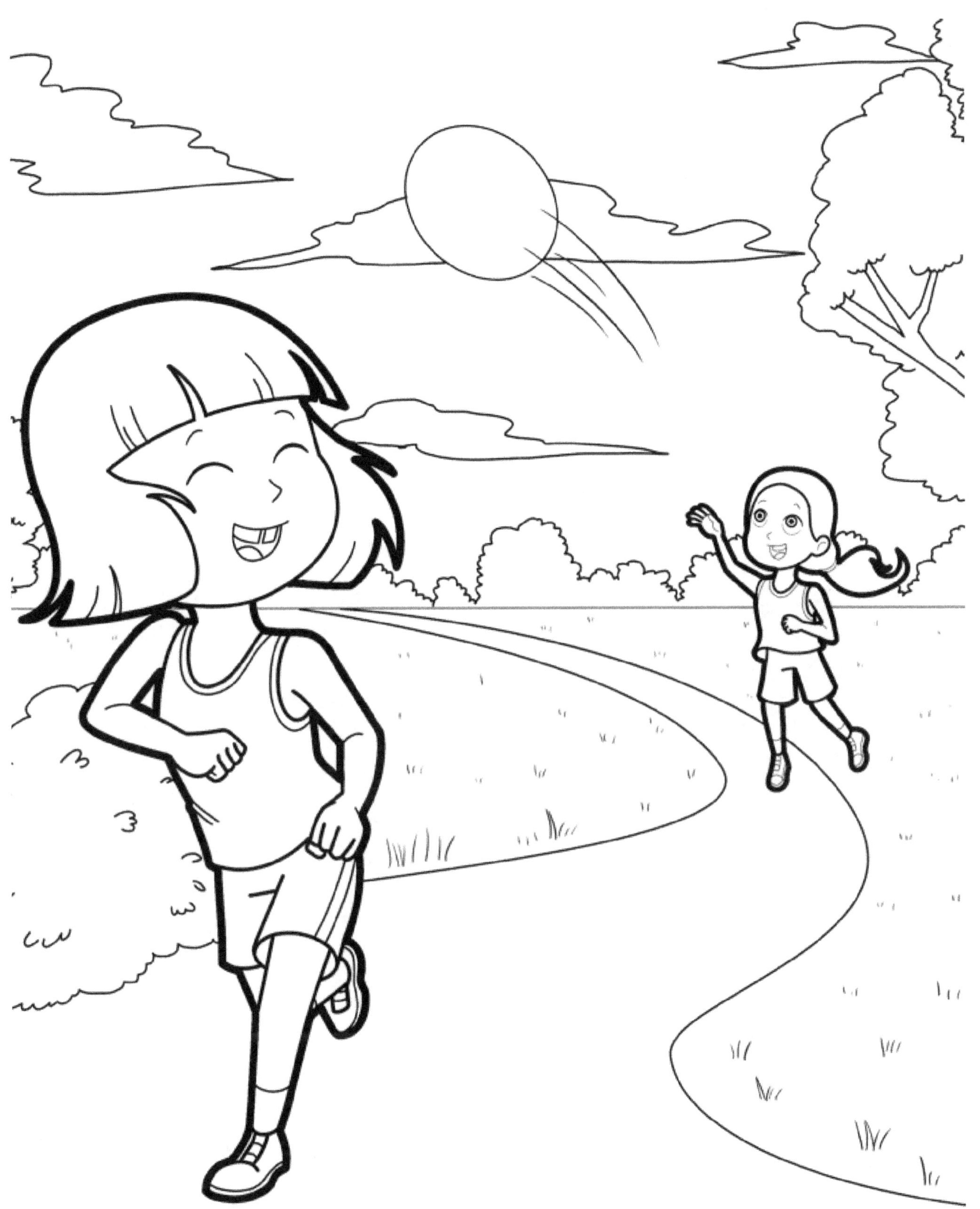

Practice writing by tracing the phrase below.

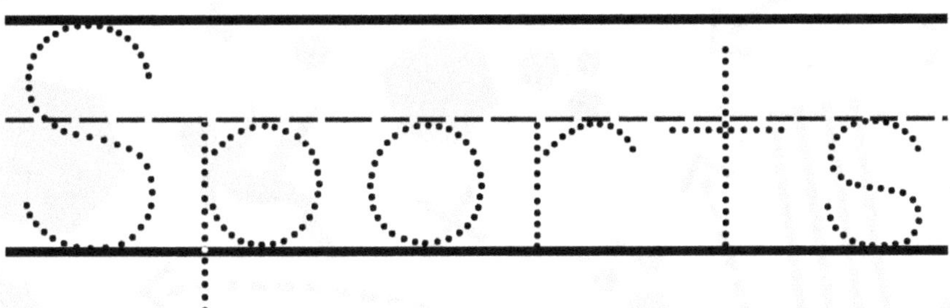

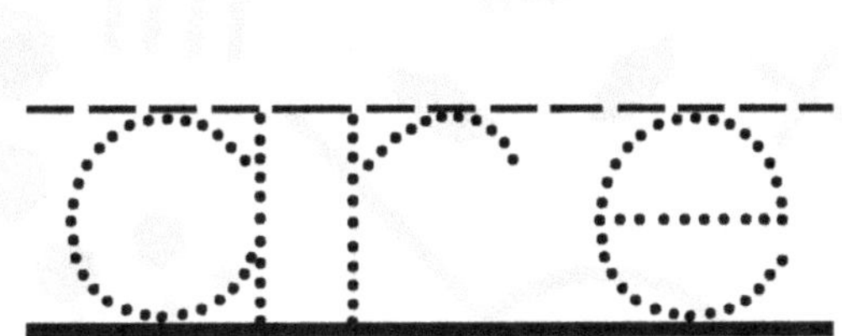

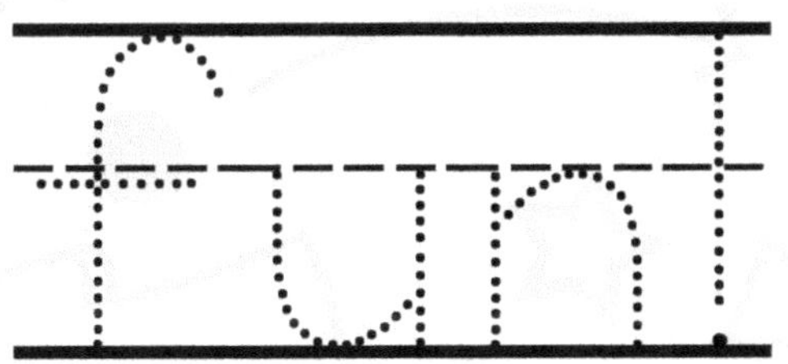

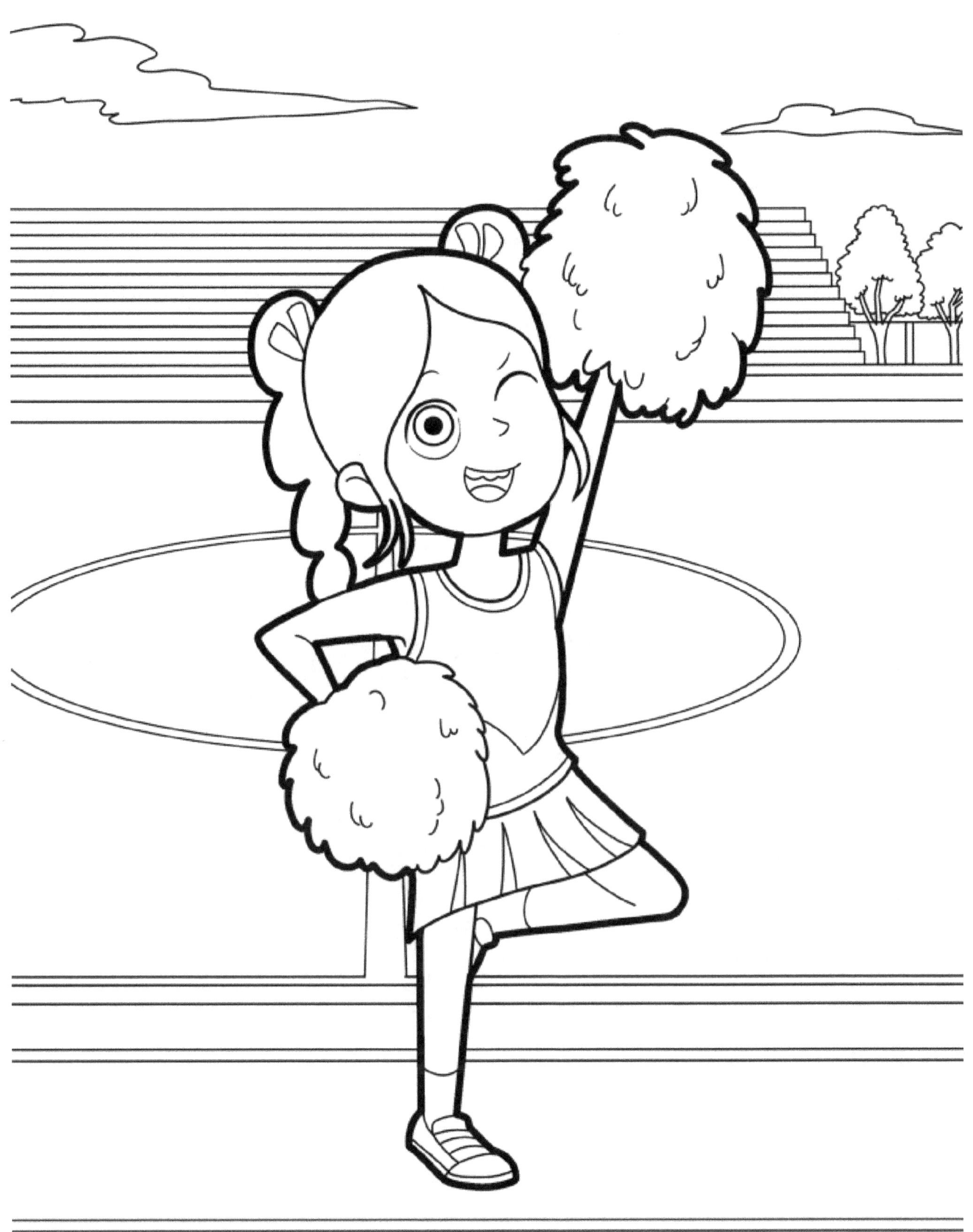

Circle the picture that does not belong in the row.

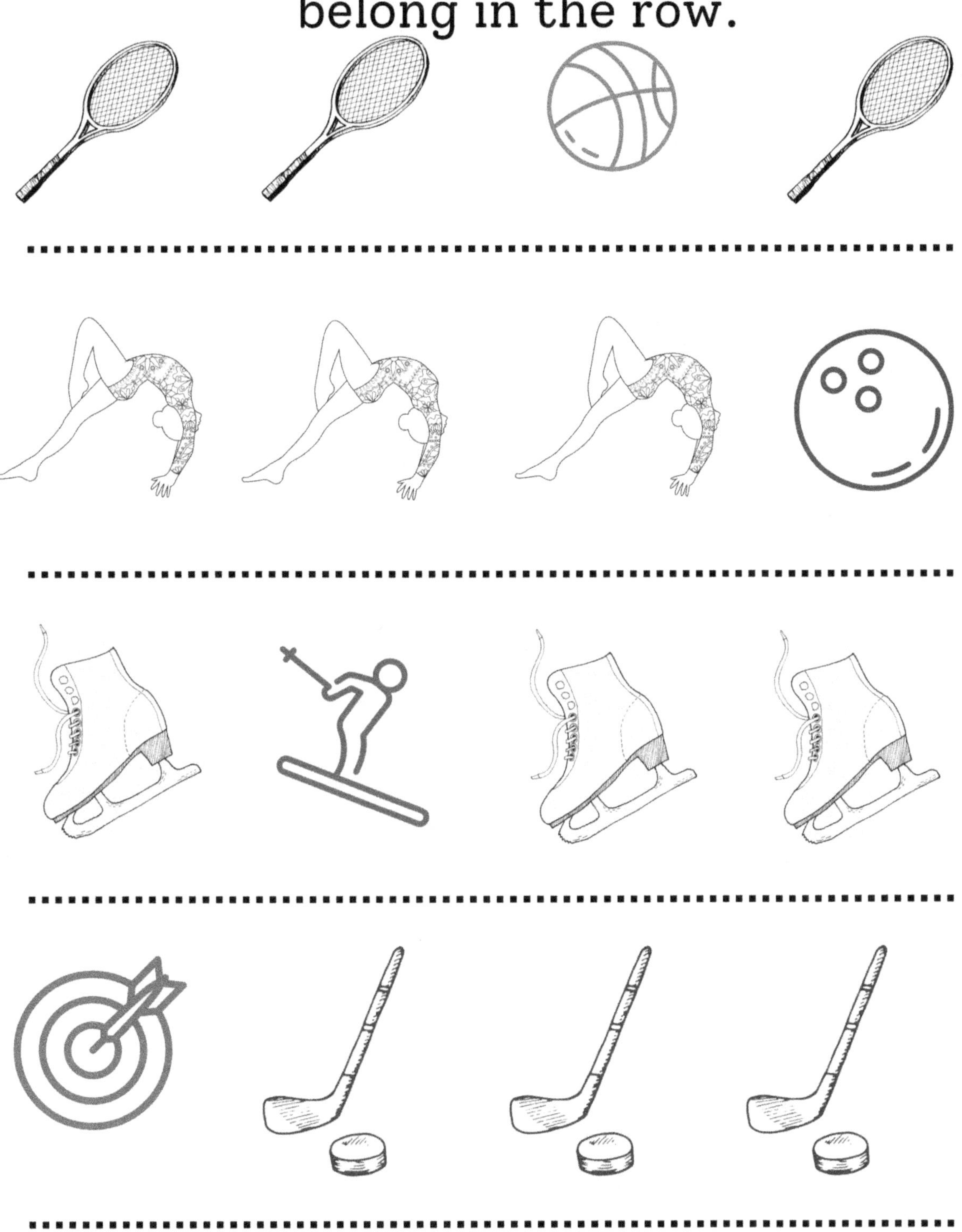

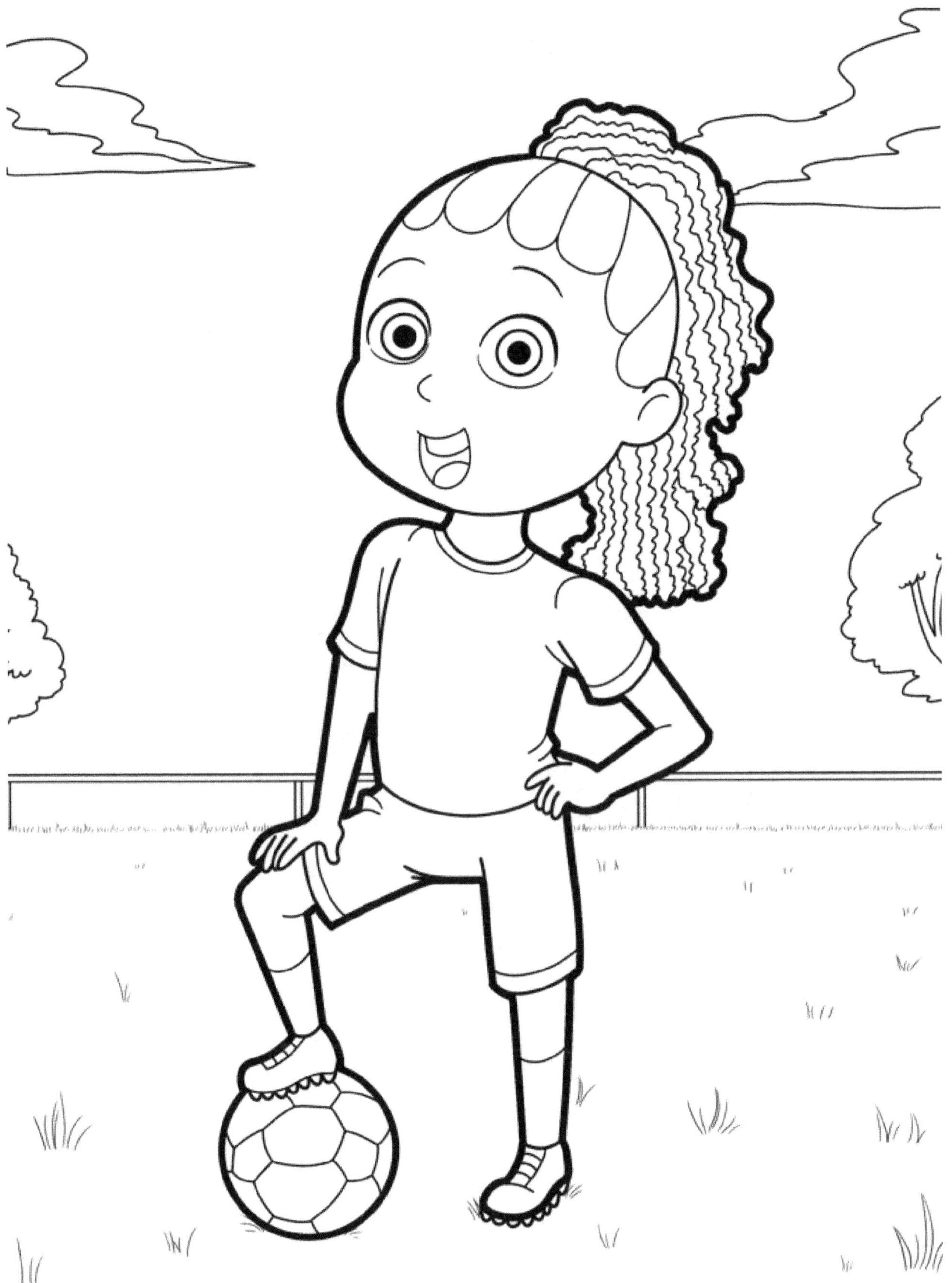

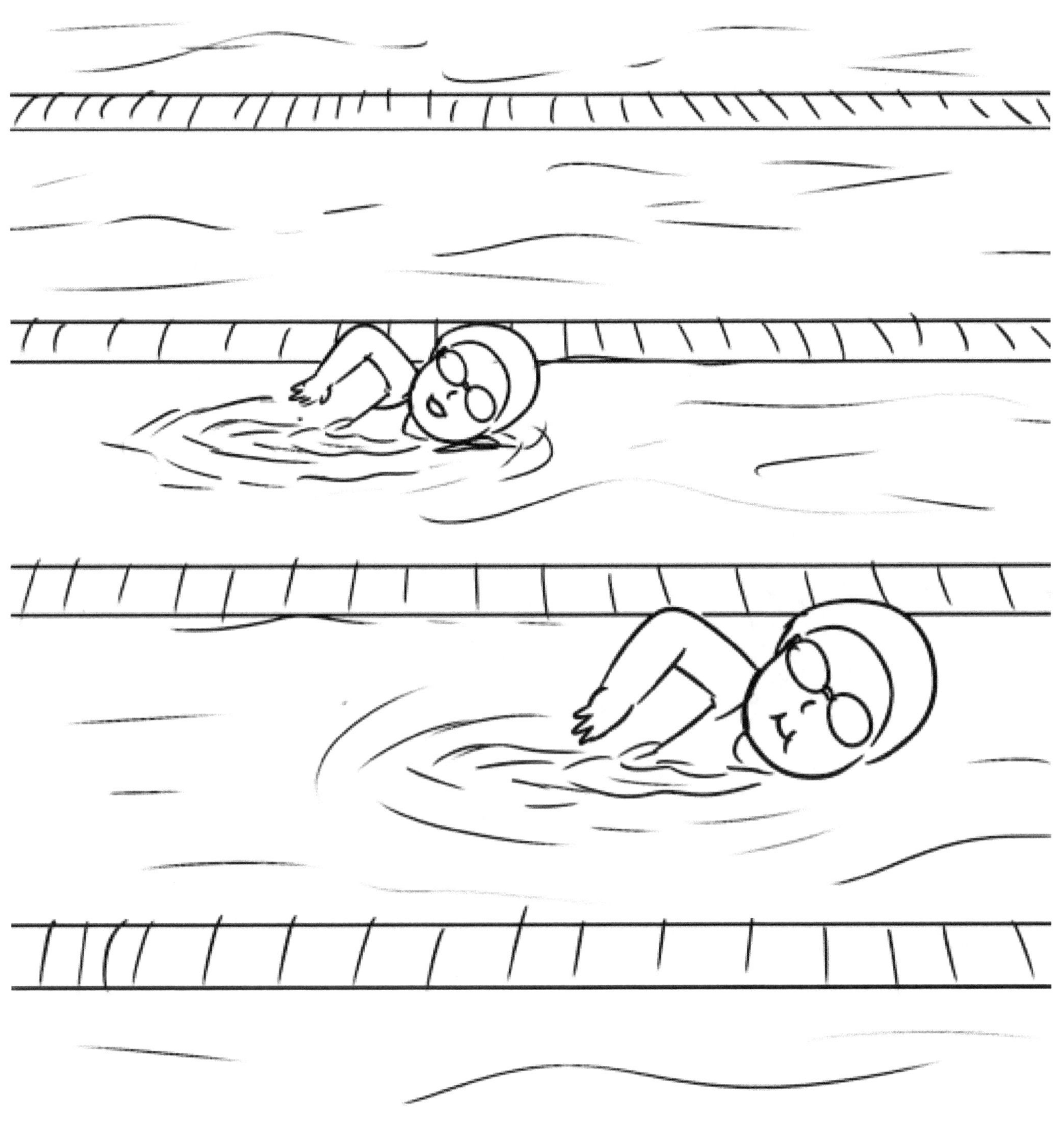

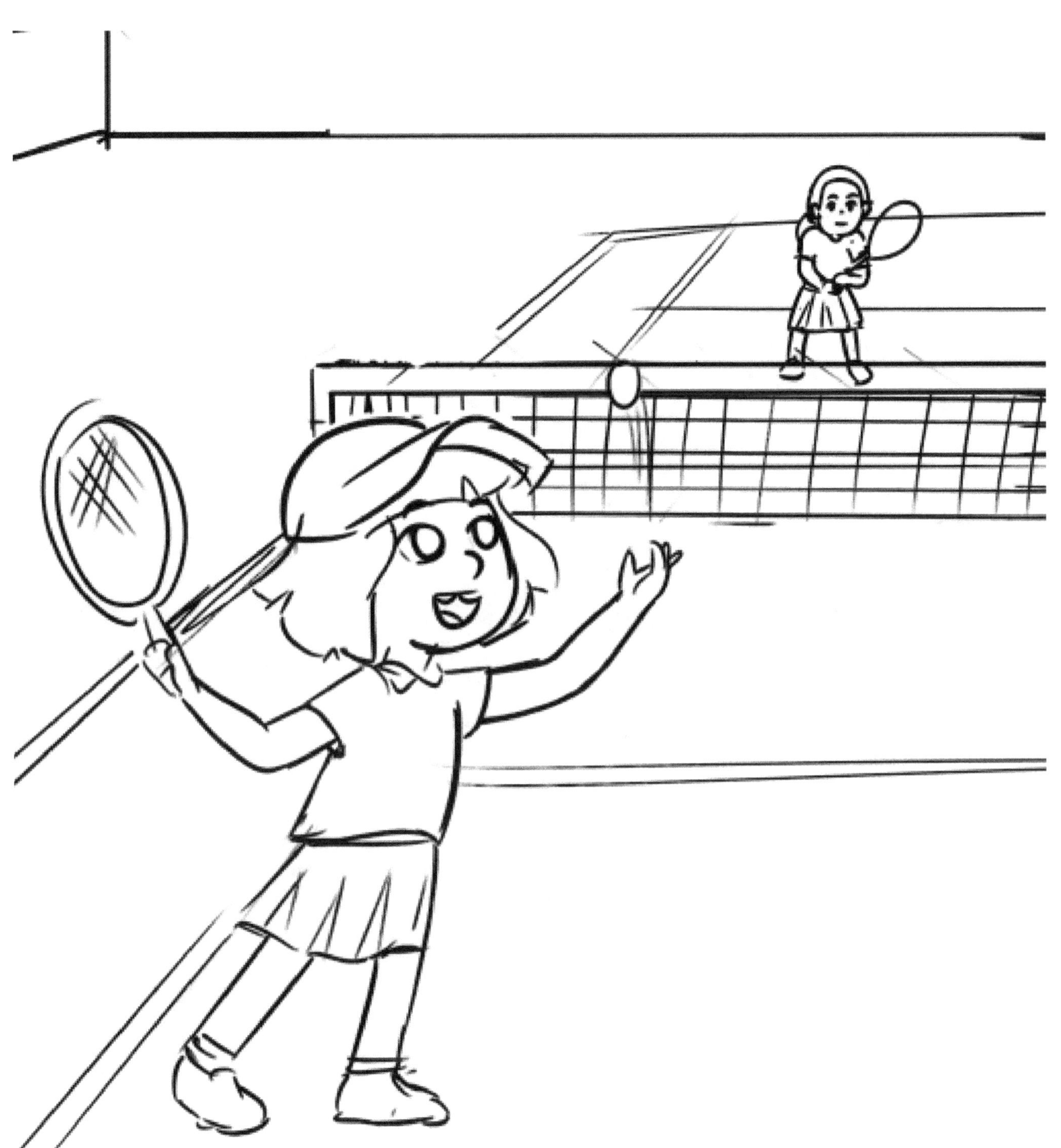

Practice writing the word below.

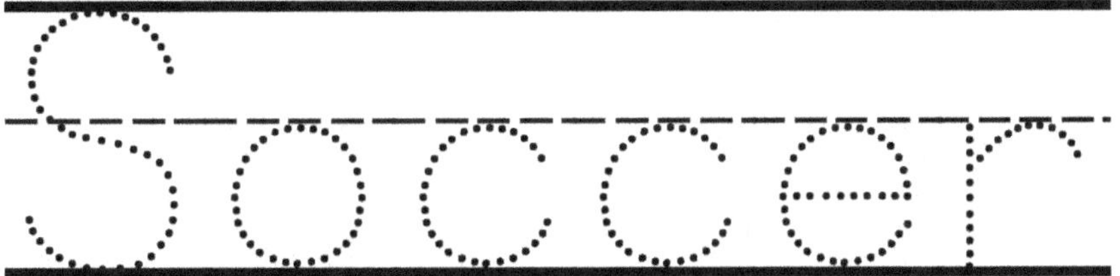

Color the soccer ball with your own style!

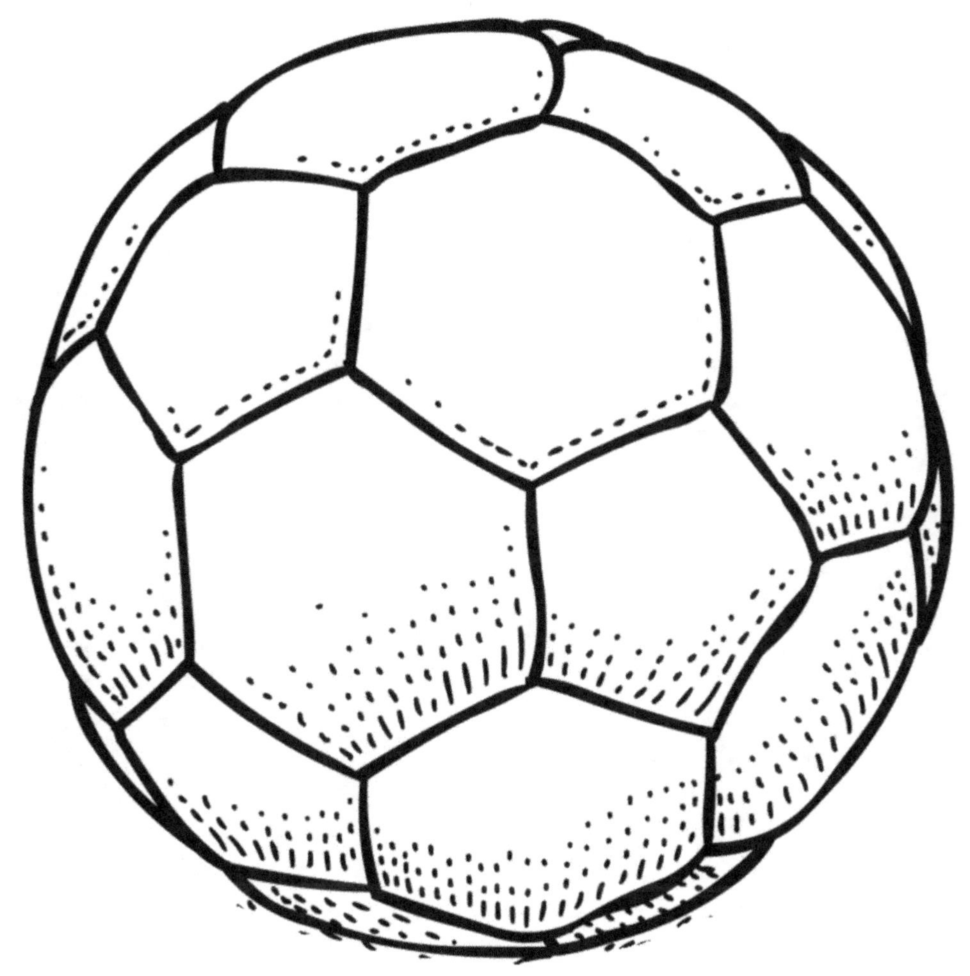

Tic Tac Toe

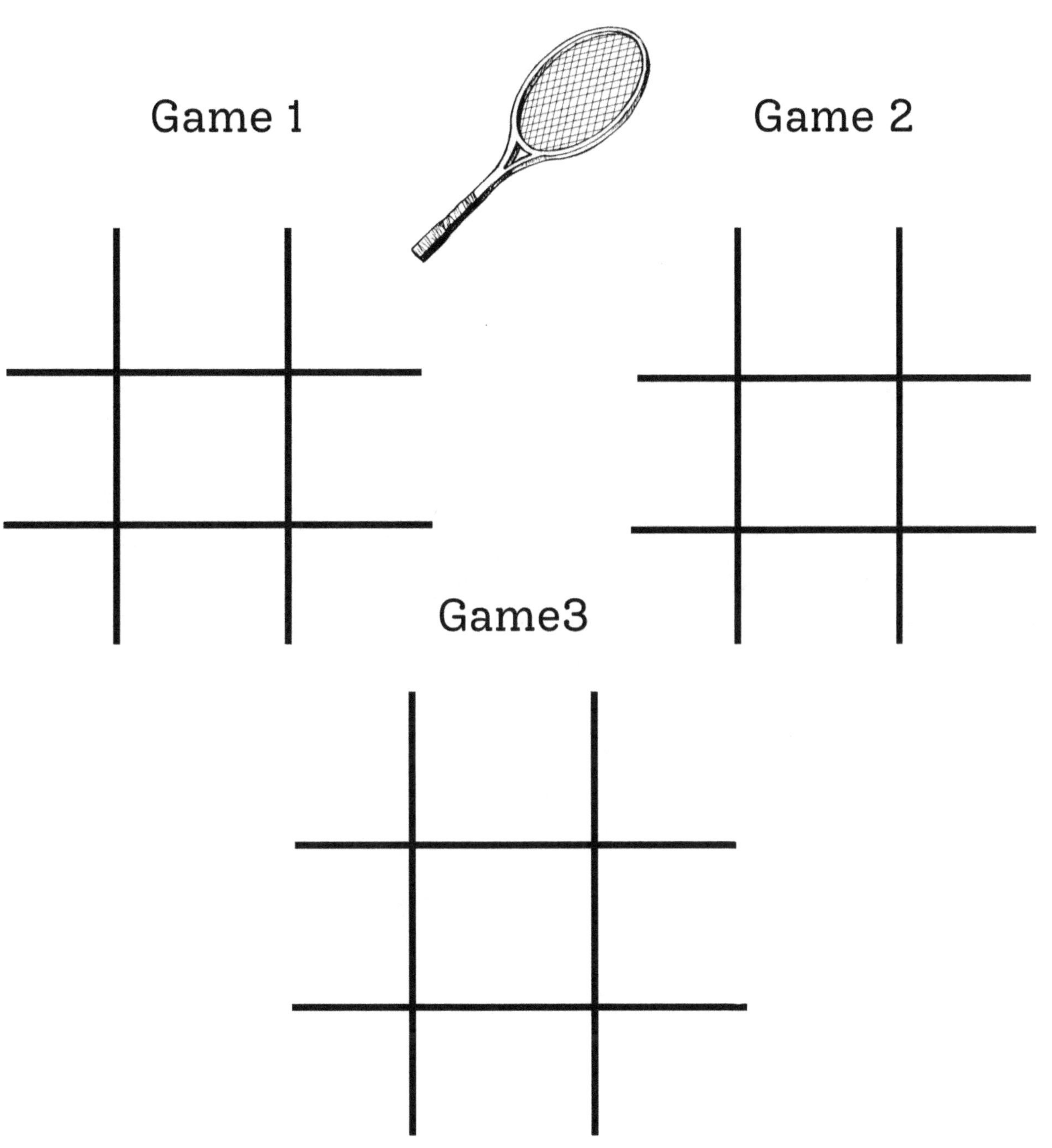

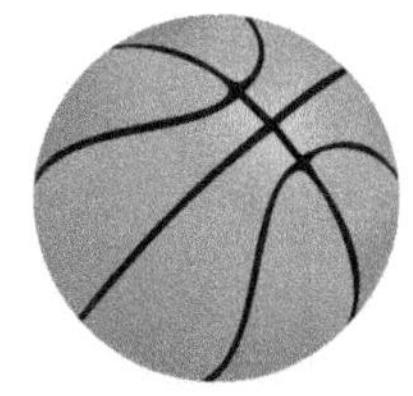

ABOUT THE AUTHOR

Ashleigh is a former collegiate basketball player

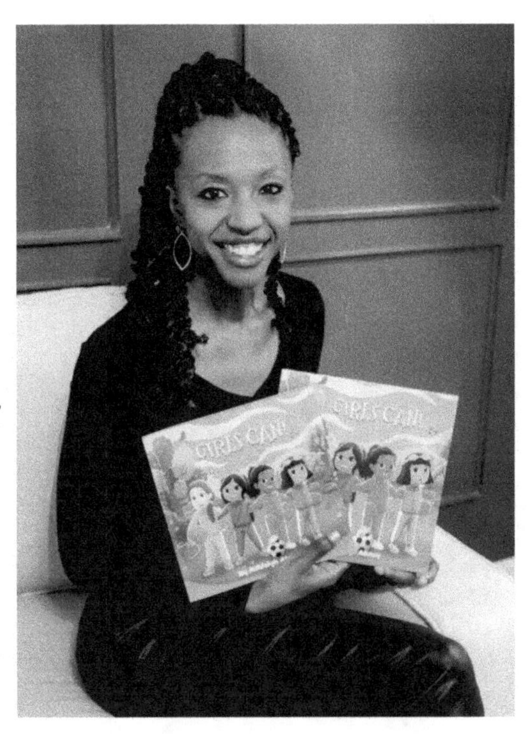

As a mom, I am incredibly passionate about the benefits sports offers children. At a young age, through sports, children have the opportunity to learn leadership skills, confidence, teamwork, and can begin building a foundation for a strong work ethic.

Please visit the Empower Books website empowerbooksforkids.net or visit us on social media Instagram: @empowerbooks

www.ingramcontent.com/pod-product-compliance
Lightning Source LLC
LaVergne TN
LVHW061254100826
845148LV00008B/1119

9798987026625